Student Support
Materials for
Edexcel AS History

Unit 1 D3

Russia in revolution, 1881–1924:
From autocracy to dictatorship

Series editor: Angela Leonard

Authors: Alan White and Ben Gregory

William Collins' dream of knowledge for all began with the publication of his first book in 1819. A self-educated mill worker, he not only enriched millions of lives, but also founded a flourishing publishing house. Today, staying true to this spirit, Collins books are packed with inspiration, innovation and practical expertise. They place you at the centre of a world of possibility and give you exactly what you need to explore it.

Collins. Freedom to teach

Published by Collins
An imprint of HarperCollins*Publishers*
77 – 85 Fulham Palace Road
Hammersmith
London
W6 8JB

Browse the complete Collins catalogue at
www.collinseducation.com

© HarperCollins*Publishers* Limited 2012

10 9 8 7 6 5 4 3 2 1

ISBN-13 978 0 00 745739 7

Alan White and Ben Gregory assert their moral rights to be identified as the authors of this work

British Library Cataloguing in Publication Data
A Catalogue record for this publication is available from the British Library

Commissioned by Andrew Campbell
Project managed by Alexandra Riley and Shirley Wakley
Additional project management by Charlie Evans
Production by Simon Moore

Designed by Jouve
Edited by Michael Upchurch and Sara Wiegand
Proofread by Joan Miller
Indexed by Michael Forder
Illustrations by Ann Paganuzzi
Picture research and text by Grace Glendinning and Caroline Green
Cover picture research by Caroline Green
Cover design by Angela English
Technical review by Peter Callaghan

Printed and bound by Printing Express Limited, Hong Kong

Cover Acknowledgement: *The Bolshevik* by Boris Mikhailovich Kustodiev, 1920.

Acknowledgements
The publishers gratefully acknowledge the permission granted to reproduce the copyright material in this book. While every effort has been made to trace and contact copyright holders, where this has not been possible the publishers will be pleased to make the necessary arrangements at the first opportunity.

pp 24, 32 & 40 from *A People's Tragedy: The Russian Revolution 1891–1924* by Orlando Figes, published by Pimlico, and Viking Penguin in the US. Reprinted by permission of The Random House Group Limited; pp 34, 46, 49 & 57 Public Domain quotations used courtesy of the Marxists Internet Archive; p 35 *from The Making of Eastern Europe by* Philip Longworth (Copyright © Philip Longworth, 1965) Reprinted by permission of A.M. Heath & Co Ltd.; p 36 from *A History of Russia, by* N. Riasanovsky & M. Steinberg (2005) © Oxford University Press; p 48 from *Diary in Exile* by Leon Trotsky (1958) © Harvard University Press; p 62 from Alan M. Ball, *Russia's Last Capitalists: The Nepmen, 1921–1929* © 1990 by the Regents of the University of California. Published by the University of California Press; p 65 from Robert Service, *Did Lenin lead to Stalin?* © International Socialism 55 (Summer 1992).

The publisher would like to thank the following for permission to reproduce pictures in these pages:

COVER: *The Bolshevik* by Boris Mikhailovich Kustodiev, 1920. Used courtesy of Photos 12/Alamy; p 80 Library of Congress/George Grantham Bain collection/WikiMedia Commons.

MIX
Paper from responsible sources
FSC™ C007454

FSC™ is a non-profit international organisation established to promote the responsible management of the world's forests. Products carrying the FSC label are independently certified to assure consumers that they come from forests that are managed to meet the social, economic and ecological needs of present and future generations, and other controlled sources.

Find out more about HarperCollins and the environment at
www.harpercollins.co.uk/green

Contents

Introduction: The Russian Empire in 1881
4–7

The Russian Empire: land and people   4   The nature of the Tsarist regime   6

Challenges to the Tsarist State, 1881–1906
8–27

Alexander III: repression and counter-reform   8   Opposition groups and parties   17
Peasant Russia before the 1905 Revolution   10   Opposition groups: Liberals   18
Economic changes: industrialisation   12   Opposition parties: the Socialist Revolutionaries   18
Economic changes: the role of Witte   14   Opposition parties: Social Democrats   20
The growth of opposition to Tsarism   16   The 1905 Revolution   22

Tsarism's last chance: 1906–17
28–39

Repression in rural Russia in and after 1905   28   The impact of war, 1914–7   36
Reform and its impact, 1906–14   30   The February/March Revolution, 1917:
Continuity and change in Russia, 1881–1914   34   the downfall of the Romanovs   38

February to October 1917
40–49

The Provisional Government and its problems   40   The October/November Revolution, 1917   46
Lenin and the April Theses   42   Why the Bolsheviks were able to seize power
The July Days and the Kornilov affair   44   in October 1917   48

The Bolshevik consolidation of power, 1918–24
50–67

The Bolsheviks in power: first steps, 1917–8   50   From War Communism to the NEP   60
The Civil War   52   NEP Russia, 1921–4   62
Why did the Bolsheviks win the Civil War?   58   Three key institutions: Party, secret police, Red Army   66

Exam skills
68–91

Introduction   68   Structuring and writing an effective answer   80
Working out the focus of the question   68   Key tips   83
Recognising the different types of question   70   Understanding the mark scheme   85
Choosing the best question to tackle   79   Preparing for the exam   88

Questions and answers
92–116

Question 1: The Bolsheviks' success in November 1917   92   Question 3: Why the Bolsheviks stayed in
Question 2: Changes in the Russian economy,   power in 1924   103
1881–1914   97   Question 4: The most important result
   of the 1905 Revolution   109

Index
116–120

The Russian Empire: land and people

Basic geography

The late 19th-century Russian Empire was geographically the largest country in the world. Its land area was more than twice that of the United States and ninety times bigger than the United Kingdom. A further illustration of Russia's vastness was the fact that the Trans-Siberian Railway, which opened in 1905 and linked Moscow with Vladivostok, crossed eight time zones.

The Russian Empire straddled Europe and Asia, with the Ural Mountains acting as the dividing line between the two. Asiatic Russia, which included Siberia, lay to the east of the Urals and consisted mostly of forest and steppe (grassland). Siberia was sparsely populated and economically under-developed. European Russia, to the west of the Urals, contained the Russian Empire's most fertile agricultural area – the 'Black Earth' region – and almost all of its major towns and cities.

The Russian Empire: geography

Population growth and distribution

In the 19th and early 20th centuries, Russia's population was growing at a faster rate than that of any other European country. In 1815 the population of the Russian Empire was 45 million. By 1914 it was 170 million.

This explosive population growth put the agricultural sector of the Russian economy under intense pressure. Food production struggled to keep pace with demand. Many Russians barely managed to survive, with famine an ever-present threat.

Population growth was not accompanied by an enormous surge of people into Russia's towns. Late 19th-century Russia remained an overwhelmingly rural country. In the 1880s more than 80 per cent of the population lived in the countryside, many people living in small, one-street villages. The 1897 census showed that only two of the Empire's cities had a population of more than a million – St Petersburg, the capital, and Moscow – and only 16 other towns and cities had a population of more than 100 000.

Nationalities

The Russian Empire was a multi-national state – that is, a state containing people of many different nationalities. Russians were the largest single nationality within the Empire, but overall they were outnumbered by non-Russians. The multi-national character of the Russian Empire had important consequences. Among the Empire's non-Russians were those who resented living under what they saw as alien Russian rule. From the point of view of the Tsarist regime, the most troublesome nationality were the Poles. There were Polish uprisings against Russian rule in 1830–1 and in 1863–4. On both occasions the uprisings were suppressed but Poland's thirst for independence remained strong.

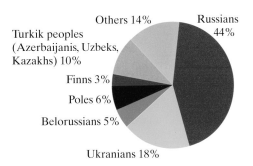

Nationalities within the Russian Empire, 1897

Social classes

At the top of the late 19th-century social pyramid were the Tsar and the Russian nobility. Beneath them was a small middle class – businessmen, industrialists and professional people such as doctors and lawyers – which accounted for around 10 per cent of the total population. Even smaller was Russia's industrial working class. The snapshot given in Russia's 1897 census suggested that only two to three per cent of the population were industrial workers. The vast majority of late 19th-century Russians – more than 80 per cent of the total – were peasants engaged in subsistence farming.

Religion

The Russian Empire was a land in which many religions were practised. There were Catholics and Jews in Poland; Protestants in Finland and the Baltic provinces; and Sunni and Shia Moslems in Asiatic Russia. The biggest and most influential religious organisation within the Empire, however, was the Russian Orthodox Church.

The Russian Orthodox Church was very closely identified with the Tsarist regime. Its head, the Chief Procurator of the Holy Synod, was appointed by the Tsar. This had been the case since the reign of Peter the Great (1682–1725).

Essential notes

Peasants owned or rented the land they worked. They were not agricultural labourers who, by contrast, were paid a wage by an employer.

Essential notes

The Russian Orthodox Church was the largest of the Orthodox churches. These became distinct from the Roman Catholic Church in the Middle Ages. The Orthodox churches have their own theology and rituals, though their core beliefs are the same as those of other Christian churches.

The nature of the Tsarist regime

Origins of the Russian Empire

In the mid-16th century Ivan ('the Terrible'), Grand Duke of Moscow, dispensed with his existing title and crowned himself Tsar, or Emperor, of Russia. In 1613 the title of Tsar passed to Michael Romanov, the first of the Romanov dynasty that was destined to rule Russia for the next 300 years. In the 17th and 18th centuries the Russian Empire grew in power, in particular, during the reigns of Peter the Great (1682–1725) and Catherine the Great (1762–96).

Autocracy

The Russian Empire was an autocracy throughout its existence. Even by the late 19th century there were no formal checks of any kind on the Tsar's power:

- There was no constitution setting out what the Tsar could and could not do.

- There was no assembly containing elected representatives of the people that had a right to be involved in the process of making the law.

- There were no legal safeguards protecting the rights and freedoms of citizens.

In the late 19th century, Russia was governed on a day-to-day basis by ministers appointed by the Tsar and by civil servants working in ministers' departments. The most important government departments were the ministries of the Interior, Foreign Affairs, War and Finance.

Government ministers reported to the Tsar on an individual basis. They did not (before 1905) meet as a group to plan the government's overall strategy. There was (again before 1905) no chief minister who coordinated the work of the government as a whole. Much depended on the personal qualities of individual Tsars.

Russia in 1881

Alexander II (Tsar, 1855–81) was not an instinctive reformer, but defeat in the Crimean War of the 1850s convinced him that Russia had to modernise if it was to remain a major power. The result was the so-called 'Great Reforms' of the 1860s.

- Under the Emancipation Statutes (1861) serfs owned by landowners won their legal freedom (see pages 10–11, for more detail on the emancipation of the serfs).

- Local government reform (1864) saw the establishment of elected local assemblies, the *zemstva* (singular: *zemstvo*), in Russia's districts and provinces. Responsibilities of the *zemstva* included education, health and road-building. Electoral arrangements for the *zemstva* were heavily weighted in favour of the nobility and upper classes.

- Judicial reform (1864) gave judges greater independence from government control and also introduced trial by jury in major criminal cases.

Essential notes

An autocracy is a state in which one individual has supreme and unlimited power.

Examiners' notes

You would not be asked about the 'Great Reforms' directly in the examination, but you need to be aware of them because they were a feature of the political environment in which Alexander III and Nicholas II operated.

- Education reform improved access to higher education, increased student numbers and gave universities more control over their own affairs.

- Censorship became less strict after 1865, with publishers no longer being required to submit material to government censors before publication. Freedom of expression remained limited, though, because it was still an offence to publish anything the authorities viewed as unacceptable.

- Military reform (1863–75) involved improvements in officer training, radical changes to the conscription system and abolition of corporal punishment in the Russian army.

Alexander II was assassinated in 1881 by revolutionaries calling themselves the 'People's Will'. Both of his successors as Tsar, Alexander III (1881–94) and Nicholas II (1894–1917), were, by contrast, strong anti-reformers.

The pillars of Tsarism

The main pillars of Tsarism – those institutions that assisted the Romanov dynasty in maintaining its hold on Russia – were the bureaucracy, the secret police, the army, the Russian nobility and the Orthodox Church. These institutions may have looked imposing and powerful from the outside, but each had its weaknesses.

Essential notes

It is customary and entirely acceptable to refer to the secret police in late Tsarist Russia as the *Okhrana*. Strictly speaking, though, the *Okhrana* were specialist counter-revolutionary units within the secret police – and were thus only part of the secret police force, not the whole of it.

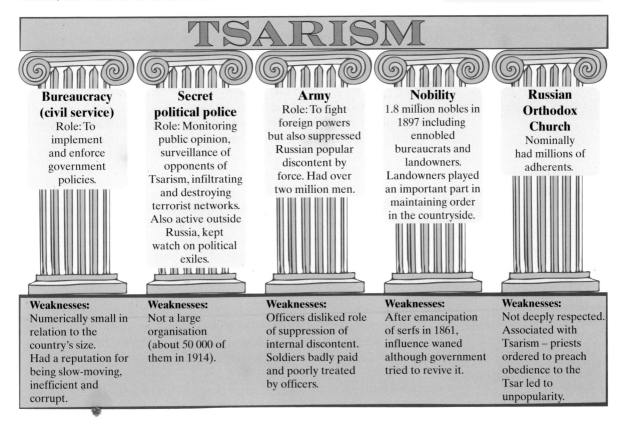

Bureaucracy (civil service)	Secret political police	Army	Nobility	Russian Orthodox Church
Role: To implement and enforce government policies.	Role: Monitoring public opinion, surveillance of opponents of Tsarism, infiltrating and destroying terrorist networks. Also active outside Russia, kept watch on political exiles.	Role: To fight foreign powers but also suppressed Russian popular discontent by force. Had over two million men.	1.8 million nobles in 1897 including ennobled bureaucrats and landowners. Landowners played an important part in maintaining order in the countryside.	Nominally had millions of adherents.
Weaknesses: Numerically small in relation to the country's size. Had a reputation for being slow-moving, inefficient and corrupt.	**Weaknesses:** Not a large organisation (about 50 000 of them in 1914).	**Weaknesses:** Officers disliked role of suppression of internal discontent. Soldiers badly paid and poorly treated by officers.	**Weaknesses:** After emancipation of serfs in 1861, influence waned although government tried to revive it.	**Weaknesses:** Not deeply respected. Associated with Tsarism – priests ordered to preach obedience to the Tsar led to unpopularity.

The pillars of Tsarism: features and weaknesses

Alexander III: repression and counter-reform

Alexander III was a giant of a man, well over 6 feet tall and immensely strong physically. He had a forceful, determined personality but lacked intelligence and imagination.

Like his father, Alexander III was intent on preserving Russia's status as a major European power. As a result he wanted to see Russia develop its industrial potential and he led his country into an alliance with France in 1894.

In other ways, though, Alexander III was an ultra-conservative. He pursued a policy of what has been called 'counter-reform'. Counter-reform was partly a reaction to the murder of Alexander II, but Alexander III also believed that his father's 'Great Reforms' had been a mistake, weakening Tsarism and leaving it insecure. His policy was to undo the reforms as far as possible.

Pobedonostev

Alexander III's views on the 1860s reforms owed much to the influence of his chief adviser, Konstantin Pobedonostev. Pobedonostev was an uncompromising conservative whose views were based on a deeply pessimistic view of human nature. He believed that human beings were by instinct brutal and could only be kept under control by the twin forces of religion and firm autocratic government.

Counter-reform

Just before his death, Alexander II had approved a plan for the reform of central government worked out by his Interior Minister, Count Mikhail Loris-Melikov.

Loris-Melikov believed that Tsarism could best guarantee its future by making modest concessions to its critics. His plan involved the establishment of two new government commissions which were to have an advisory role in relation to proposed new laws. These commissions were to include elected *zemstvo* members. Loris-Melikov's scheme thus opened the way to elected representatives contributing to central government decision-making in Russia for the first time.

This was a prospect which alarmed Alexander III. His first major decision as Tsar in 1881 was to throw out the Loris-Melikov plan, modest and limited though it was. Loris-Melikov resigned as Interior Minister. The tone of Alexander III's reign had been set.

In late 1881, 'Temporary Laws' were introduced giving Tsarist officials far-reaching emergency powers in any part of the Empire where public order was felt to be in danger. These included the power to detain individuals without trial and the power to ban public gatherings. These 'Temporary Laws' were in force in many Russian provinces throughout the period 1881–1905, and after 1905 they were applied across the whole country.

The new post of 'land captain' was established in 1889. The land captains, recruited from among the nobility, were given powers to direct and control peasant affairs in their areas. They replaced the *zemstva* magistrates who had previously done this work.

The regime was suspicious of representative institutions in any form. As a result, local government was reshaped by the *Zemstvo* Statute (1890). Provincial governors were given the power to overrule *zemstvo* decisions and new rules reduced peasant representation in the *zemstvo* assemblies.

Early in Alexander III's reign, censorship was tightened, with a return to the pre-1865 system under which publishers were required to submit material to government censors before publication.

In 1884, the universities, always potential centres of unrest, lost the right to self-government which they had been given in the 1860s.

Russification

The Tsarist regime was acutely conscious of the threat to the stability of the Russian Empire posed by its minority nationalities. An attempt was made to diminish this threat in the reign of Alexander III through a policy of 'Russification'. This involved seeking to impose Russia's language, religion and culture on non-Russians:

- In Poland, the Ukraine and the Baltic provinces, Russian became the language in which lessons were delivered in schools and cases were heard in law courts – despite the fact it was not the native language of most people in these places.

- The Russian Orthodox Church was given government subsidies to undertake missionary work aimed at winning over non-Russians to its doctrines.

Russification aroused much resentment among the minority nationalities.

Anti-Semitism

No minority nationality suffered as much at the hands of Tsarism as Russia's Jews. Anti-Semitism was rife in all levels of Russian society in the early 19th century, but in the 1880s it became government policy to a greater extent than ever before. The 'May Laws' (1882) restricted Jewish access to higher education, banned Jews from settling in rural areas and denied Jews the right to vote in *zemstvo* elections.

When anti-Semitic pogroms took place in the area known as the 'Pale of Settlement' in the western part of European Russia in the early 1880s, the authorities were in no hurry to put a stop to them and may even have discreetly encouraged them. Small wonder that two million Jews left Russia, mostly for the United States, between 1881 and 1914.

Essential notes

The Empire's Jewish population, acquired when Russia won control of most of Poland in the late 18th century, numbered about four million in 1881. Virtually all of Russia's Jews lived in the 'Pale of Settlement' in western European Russia.

Essential notes

A pogrom is an organised attack on a whole community involving murder, assault and the destruction of property.

Examiners' notes

An understanding of peasant conditions and peasant grievances is essential if you are to appreciate why the peasantry were an important element in the challenge to Tsarism in 1905 – and if you are to make sense of Stolypin's post-1905 land reforms.

Essential notes

Pre-1861 Russian serfs were not simply slaves. They could be bought and sold by their owners, but they did have some rights in law. There was, for example, a law which limited the number of days each week they had to work for their owners.

Essential notes

Crop rotation was designed to ensure that the soil retained its fertility. This was achieved by leaving areas uncultivated, or fallow, every third year. The three-year system of crop rotation used in Russia was antiquated: in western Europe it had been abandoned in favour of more sophisticated systems of rotation and greater use of fertilisers.

Peasant Russia before the 1905 Revolution

The peasantry

Russia's rural population in the late 19th century was varied. It included landowners, clergymen, herdsmen, forestry workers and fishermen. However, by far the biggest group within the rural population was the peasantry – small-scale subsistence farmers. Before 1861 around half the peasantry were 'state peasants', mostly farming state-owned land in the northern districts of Russia and in Siberia, and half were serfs owned by private landowners. The heartland of serfdom was central and southern European Russia.

Before emancipation, serf owners typically made a proportion of the land on their estates available to their serfs to cultivate for subsistence purposes. Legally, though, the serfs' land remained the property of the landowner. In return for the land they received, serfs were required to work for their owners on the part of their estates the latter kept for themselves. This labour service normally involved around three days' work each week.

In 1861 serfs were emancipated with the land they had traditionally cultivated but they were not given it free of charge. The 1861 land transfer arrangements involved the state compensating serf-owners for the land they had lost with government bonds, and recovering its outlay from the liberated serfs over a scheduled 49-year period in the form of 'redemption payments'. Later, in 1886, a similar 'redemption' process was started to enable state peasants to buy land they had previously rented.

Peasant farming

Strip farming was the norm in Russian villages.

- The land used for growing crops was divided into three sections or 'open fields'.

- Each peasant household had strips in each of the sections. Historian Richard Pipes describes these strips as being 9 to 12 feet (3 to 4 metres) wide and several hundred yards (metres) in length. A household, he suggests, might typically have had 30–50 strips in total, but the exact number depended on the size of the household.

- Each household farmed its own strips but had to conform to village-wide arrangements for crop rotation.

	Year 1	Year 2	Year 3
Area 1	Wheat or rye	Oats	Fallow
Area 2	Oats	Fallow	Wheat or rye
Area 3	Fallow	Wheat or rye	Oats

Crop rotation arrangements of the kind typically used in a late 19th-century Russian village

The purpose of the strip system was to ensure a fair distribution of land between households. The concern with fairness was such that in most Russian villages there was a wholesale redistribution of strips every 10–15 years. This practice continued after emancipation.

Strip farming was inefficient. Only two-thirds of available land was under cultivation in any one growing season, time was wasted moving from strip to strip and periodic redistribution of strips meant that households had no real incentive to improve their land. These inefficiencies go a long way towards explaining why crop yields in Russia were low in comparison with western Europe. Of course, environmental factors need to be borne in mind too: outside the fertile Black Earth region soils were poor and the growing season short.

The *mir*

The village commune, or *mir*, was a uniquely Russian institution. It was an assembly made up of the heads of each household in each village. The core functions of the *mir* were to decide on matters relating to the distribution of land and to fix the dates of key arable operations such as harvesting. The *mir* also regulated village life in a number of other ways:

- It was responsible for the collection of taxes and redemption payments.

- It was expected to maintain order within the village.

- It selected conscripts for military service.

The *mir* existed before 1861 but the additional responsibilities it was given under the emancipation arrangements increased its influence.

Increasing peasant discontent

In the late 19th century, peasant conditions worsened and discontent increased. Three main factors were at work: population growth, taxation and redemption payments.

1. Explosive population growth in the late 19th century gave rise to intense 'land hunger' among the peasantry. In the 1870s and 1880s much of the peasantry had less land than was needed for basic subsistence. Millions of peasants had to take on extra work, usually as agricultural labourers on nobles' estates, in order to make ends meet. The obstacle in the way of acquiring the additional land these peasants craved was lack of money. Some help was available through the Peasant Land Bank, established in 1883, but its operations were limited.

2. The burden of taxation became heavier. The Tsarist regime, needing money to finance railway-building, increased taxes on commodities the peasants could not produce for themselves and therefore had to buy, notably sugar, tea, tobacco, vodka, matches and heating oil.

3. Redemption payments were a grievance. The payments were onerous and large numbers of peasants fell into arrears. The peasantry saw these payments as unjust in principle. Peasants believed the land they had cultivated before emancipation was theirs by right and they did not understand why they had to pay for it.

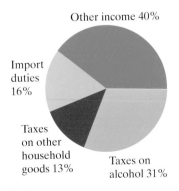

Other income 40%

Import duties 16%

Taxes on other household goods 13%

Taxes on alcohol 31%

Indirect taxes

Essential notes

A society's human capital can be defined as the stock of economically valuable knowledge, skills and experience possessed by its members.

Economic changes: industrialisation

In the mid-19th century Russia was in economic terms the most backward of the European great powers. It possessed natural resources in abundance – oil in Baku, coal and iron ore in the Ukraine, gold and silver in the Urals and Siberia – but mobilisation of these resources was in its infancy. Alexander III and Nicholas II wanted to transform Russia into a major industrial power, but there were formidable obstacles to be overcome.

Obstacles to industrial development
Shortage of capital
Mid-19th-century Russia was not awash with money which could be used to finance industrial growth. The Russian nobility, one potential source of funds, was hit by falling world food prices in the later 19th century and was struggling to farm profitably. The prosperous middle classes put their savings into banks, but Russia's middle class was small. Investment funds would have to come from elsewhere.

Human capital
The quality of Russia's human capital was modest by western European standards. Educational provision improved in the later 19th century but levels of literacy remained low. The 1897 census suggested that only one-third of the population could read. A majority of Russians thus lacked the basic levels of literacy which industrial work requires.

Poor communications
Poor internal communications were a barrier to the growth of trade and commerce. Russia's road network was primitive. In 1866 there were only 5000 km of railroads in Russia.

Food supply
Towns and cities growing as a result of industrialisation needed to be fed. Russia's antiquated system of agriculture was not equal to the task. Some late 19th- and early 20th-century Tsarist ministers, notably Witte, recognised the need to modernise agriculture but were aware that attempts at reform would encounter opposition.

Industrial development before 1906: chronology and geography
The pace of industrial growth quickened after 1861, but it was the 1890s which saw the beginnings of real industrialisation in Russia. One historian has spoken of 'the great industrial spurt of the 1890s' (Hans Rogger, *Russia in the Age of Modernisation and Revolution 1881–1917*). Industrial output doubled in the years 1892–1900. There was further sustained economic growth in the decade before the outbreak of the First World War.

Industrial development before the war was concentrated in five main areas: St Petersburg (engineering and textiles), Moscow (also engineering and textiles), the Donbas region in the Ukraine (coal, iron and steel), Baku in the Caucasus (oil) and Poland (coal and textiles).

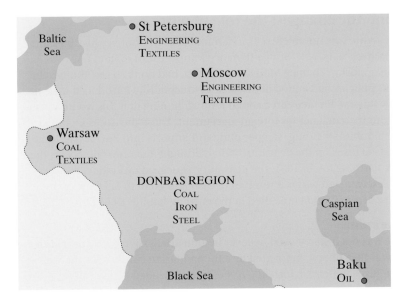

Industry in Russia before 1914

Characteristics of industrial development in Russia
State capitalism
Industry in Russia did not develop spontaneously. Instead, the process of industrialisation was driven forward by the state – that is, by Russia's rulers. Their motives were political: they feared that without industrial development Russia would fall behind other European countries in terms of military strength and would eventually lose its great power status. The outcome was a policy of 'state capitalism'. The Russian state invested heavily, for example, in the country's fast-growing railway network.

Reliance on foreign capital
The growth of industry in Russia depended very heavily on foreign capital. Something like one-third of all investment in Russian companies in the years before 1914 came from overseas. In addition many foreign-owned companies set up branches in Russia and employed Russians. There was sizeable British and American investment in Russia before 1914 but France was the biggest investor. The reasons were political. French investment in Russia helped to cement the 1894 Franco–Russian alliance.

Industrial concentration
As a latecomer among the industrial nations, Russia benefitted from being able to import the newest skills and ideas from abroad without having to develop them itself. One such idea was that industrial production was best concentrated in a relatively small number of very large companies and plants. The pre-1914 Russian economy exhibited a very high degree of concentration of this kind. An example is the Putilov engineering complex in St Petersburg, which by 1914 was the biggest industrial plant in Russia and one of the biggest in Europe. Industrial concentration in late Tsarist Russia had political consequences: big factories helped to facilitate the growth of trade unionism and political radicalism.

Essential notes

State capitalism can be defined as an economic policy under which the state owns and controls businesses but runs them on free market lines, expecting them to make a profit.

Essential notes

A striking example of foreign involvement in the industrial development of late Imperial Russia is the career of a Welsh steelmaker, John Hughes. After winning defence contracts in Russia, Hughes set up a steel plant in the Ukraine in the 1870s. The plant expanded rapidly and the settlement which grew up around it was named after him – Yuzovka. It developed into one of the Ukraine's biggest cities. It is known nowadays as Donetsk.

Essential notes

Sergei Witte (1849–1915) was the son of a provincial civil servant, born in Tbilisi, Georgia. He entered politics as Transport Minister in 1892, served as Minister of Finance (1882–1903) and as Chairman of the Council of Ministers (1905–6). Witte was late Tsarist Russia's most dynamic minister, but he made enemies easily: he was impatient, ambitious and unscrupulous.

Economic changes: the role of Witte

Sergei Witte was not the first Tsarist minister to promote industrialisation. His predecessors, N.K. Bunge (Finance Minister 1881–6) and I.A. Vyshnegradsky (Finance Minister, 1886–92), had done so too, though the latter's policies had ended in disaster. Vyshnegradsky introduced measures to put Russia's finances on a sound footing, hoping that this would make the country a magnet for foreign investment. These measures included cuts in public spending, steeper duties on imports into Russia (1891) and increased taxes on the peasantry. When drought and crop failures hit the Black Earth region in 1891, the peasantry, squeezed by Vyshnegradsky's policies, were left without reserves of cash and grain to fall back upon. A third of a million people died in the ensuing famine (1891–2).

Witte's aims

Witte was not a starry-eyed believer in industrialisation for its own sake. Nor was he a liberal, motivated by a humanitarian concern for the welfare of the Russian people. Instead, he was a hard-headed conservative who saw industrialisation as essential for strategic and political reasons.

Strategic reasons

Witte believed that Russia's backwardness left it vulnerable in a world in which industrial strength increasingly determined military power. At the top of his list of priorities were the establishment of an industrial base capable of producing high-quality armaments and improvements in Russia's transport network, which would enable troops to be moved around the country more efficiently.

Political reasons

Witte believed that enriching Russia through industrialisation would strengthen, not weaken, the Tsarist regime. A wealthy, prosperous Russia would, he maintained, be able to reduce the tax burden on the peasantry, thereby removing one of the principal sources of peasant discontent. Another perceived benefit of industrialisation was the growth of a capitalist class with a vested interest in the survival of Tsarism.

Witte's policies

Gold standard

Witte put Russia's currency, the rouble, on to the gold standard in 1897. This meant that the rouble was convertible on demand into gold. The idea was to boost international confidence in the rouble and to reassure prospective investors in Russia that they would not lose money through fluctuations in currency exchange rates. The adoption of the gold standard led to a sharp increase in the flow of foreign investment into Russia. Witte said of this in his memoirs, 'My greatest achievement as Minister of Finance... a tremendous reform.'

Essential notes

The adoption of the gold standard:

* allowed foreign investors to exchange Russian roubles for gold at any time
* fixed the value of the rouble in relation to other currencies on the gold standard.

Import duties

Witte retained the high import duties imposed by Vyshnegradsky in 1891. These import duties, or tariffs, protected developing Russian industries from low-price foreign competition.

Railways

Witte put into effect a massive programme of state-sponsored railway building, the centrepiece of which was the construction of the Trans-Siberian Railway (open to traffic in 1905, finally completed 1916).

Education

Recognising Russia's need for skilled labour, Witte was instrumental in the creation of more than a hundred technical schools and three institutes of technology.

Impact

Rates of economic growth in the Witte era were spectacular, but levels of production in Russia in 1914 remained well below those of the world's leading economies. Coal production was only one-tenth of Britain's and iron and steel output around half of Britain's.

Witte's policies contributed to urbanisation, to the expansion of the Russian middle classes and to the growth of the industrial working class. These developments, in particular the growth of the working class, weakened Tsarism. Low wages, 12-hour days, harsh factory discipline and abysmal housing left Russia's workers sullen and resentful.

Opposition to Witte

Opposition to Witte's policies came from a variety of quarters.

- Witte's policies were strongly opposed by some of his ministerial colleagues. His arch-enemy was the ultra-conservative V.K. Plehve.

- In government circles Witte was widely disliked at the personal level on account of his relatively modest social origins, his abrasive personality and his marriage to a divorcee of Jewish background (at a time when anti-Semitism was endemic in Russia).

- The landowning class, adversely affected by high import duties, was strongly anti-Witte.

- In 1903, against the background of a lull in economic growth and an outbreak of peasant disorder in southern Russia, Witte's enemies got the upper hand and persuaded Nicholas II – never as deep an admirer of Witte as Alexander III had been – to dismiss him as Finance Minister.

Essential notes

V.K. Plehve (1846–1904) was head of the *Okhrana* in the early 1880s and Minister of the Interior, 1902–4. Plehve opposed Witte's policies because they led to the growth of towns and cities, which he saw as hotbeds of radicalism and unrest. He thought the flow of capital into Russia from abroad left Russia shamefully reliant on foreigners. Plehve was assassinated in 1904.

The growth of opposition to Tsarism up to 1905

Opposition to Tsarism before 1881

Before the assassination of Alexander II, in 1881, Tsarism encountered opposition from several different groups.

Peasants

Russia had a long history of peasant uprisings. Usually they were localised, often being triggered by crop failures, and had no clear political agenda.

Nobility

The 18th and early 19th centuries saw a number of aristocratic conspiracies against individual Tsars. These were not challenges to Tsarism as such, but rather attempts by the conspirators to ensure that their favoured candidate took over as Tsar. In the late Tsarist era the nobility was generally supportive of the regime.

Intelligentsia

Opposition to Tsarism from within the educated middle classes – sometimes called the intelligentsia – first made its appearance in the 1860s and 1870s in the shape of the populist movement. Its early history was chaotic. In 1874, thousands of idealistic populists fanned out across the countryside to spread their doctrine but were met by a bewildered and indifferent peasantry. In 1876 the populists founded the 'Land and Liberty' organisation, only for it to split apart after two years. One faction (the 'People's Will') advocated the use of terrorist methods while the other (the 'Black Repartition') favoured non-violence. In 1881 the 'People's Will' assassinated Alexander II. In the repression that followed both groups were wiped out.

The growth of opposition to Tsarism after 1881

The opponents of Tsarism were scattered and driven underground by the ferocious repression following the murder of Alexander II. Then, in the 1890s they began to regroup and reorganise. The re-emergence of opposition may have owed something to the inspirational qualities of individual opposition leaders, but it owed more to the impact of government policies.

- Repression under Alexander III may have had the desired effect in the short term but it also aroused resentment and bitterness which damaged Tsarism in the longer term. To take only one example, the government's anti-Semitic policies were instrumental in bringing into existence a Jewish opposition party, the Bund, in 1897.

- Vyshnegradsky's tax increases and the government's mishandling of the 1891–2 famine further alienated an already hard-pressed and land-hungry peasantry.

- Working-class resentment arising out of poor living and working conditions led to widespread labour unrest in St Petersburg and Moscow in the 1890s.

- The universities were expanded in the late 19th century because modernising Russia needed graduate-level skills, but hostility to the authorities was widespread among university students, who were influenced by populist ideas.

Essential notes

Populism was inspired by the work of a clutch of mid-19th-century Russian political theorists, among them Alexander Herzen, Peter Lavrov and Michael Bakunin. Herzen argued that the *mir* had the potential to become the basis of a uniquely Russian form of socialism, while Lavrov and Bakunin called upon Russia's intelligentsia to go directly 'to the people' to preach the need for radical change.

Essential notes

The full name of the Bund was the General Jewish Workers' Bund (League). Its object was to further the interests of the Jewish working classes, principally to be found in Poland. Its leaders were Marxists, and for a short time (1898–1903) the Bund had close links with the Russian Social Democratic Labour Party. The Bund ceased to be a factor in Russian politics after Poland regained its independence at the end of the First World War.

Opposition groups and parties

Three political ideologies attracted a significant following in Russia in the years before 1914: liberalism, populism and Marxism. There were, however, divisions among supporters of each of the three.

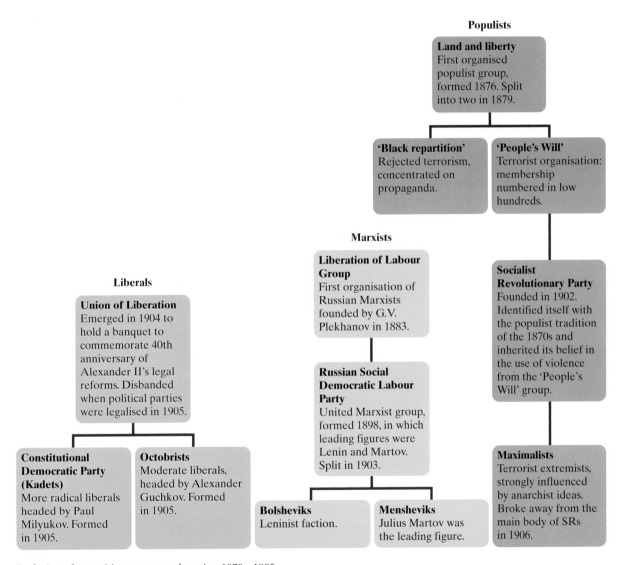

Populists

Land and liberty
First organised populist group, formed 1876. Split into two in 1879.

'Black repartition'
Rejected terrorism, concentrated on propaganda.

'People's Will'
Terrorist organisation: membership numbered in low hundreds.

Marxists

Liberation of Labour Group
First organisation of Russian Marxists founded by G.V. Plekhanov in 1883.

Socialist Revolutionary Party
Founded in 1902. Identified itself with the populist tradition of the 1870s and inherited its belief in the use of violence from the 'People's Will' group.

Liberals

Union of Liberation
Emerged in 1904 to hold a banquet to commemorate 40th anniversary of Alexander II's legal reforms. Disbanded when political parties were legalised in 1905.

Russian Social Democratic Labour Party
United Marxist group, formed 1898, in which leading figures were Lenin and Martov. Split in 1903.

Constitutional Democratic Party (Kadets)
More radical liberals headed by Paul Milyukov. Formed in 1905.

Octobrists
Moderate liberals, headed by Alexander Guchkov. Formed in 1905.

Bolsheviks
Leninist faction.

Mensheviks
Julius Martov was the leading figure.

Maximalists
Terrorist extremists, strongly influenced by anarchist ideas. Broke away from the main body of SRs in 1906.

Evolution of opposition groups and parties, 1870s–1905

☞ Continued on the next four pages

Opposition groups: Liberals

Liberalism was essentially a middle-class ideology. Its support base in late 19th-century Russia was therefore limited. Russian liberals wanted constitutional reform but opposed socialist calls for the elimination of private enterprise. The liberals' main goals were a constitution, democratic elections, representative institutions with real power and protection for basic rights and freedoms. All liberals were opposed to autocracy, but moderate liberals were prepared to see the Tsar remain in place as a constitutional monarch. Radical liberals favoured a republic. All liberals had a strong preference for non-violent methods of bringing about political change. Two liberal parties emerged after the 1905 revolution, the Constitutional Democrats (Kadets) and Octobrists.

Opposition parties: the Socialist Revolutionaries

Formation of the Socialist Revolutionary Party

The Socialist Revolutionary Party (SRs) was founded in 1902. The SRs were the heirs of the populists of the 1870s.

The SRs' principal founders were: Victor Chernov, in 1902 a political exile living in Switzerland; M.R. Gots (1886–1906), a former member of the 'People's Will' organisation; G.A. Gershuni (1870–1908); and Catherine Breshko-Breshovskaya (1844–1934), a veteran populist who as a young woman had gone directly 'to the people' to preach the need for radical change.

The Socialist Revolutionary Party aimed to be a mass party based on peasant support. At the time of its formation, however, its leadership – and almost the whole of its membership – was drawn from the middle and upper classes. Chernov was a trained lawyer and the son of a civil servant, Gots was the son of a prosperous Moscow Jewish merchant, Gershuni was a pharmacist and Breshko-Breshovskaya was the daughter of wealthy serf-owners.

Nature of the Socialist Revolutionary Party

The SRs were, from early on, a relatively loosely organised and undisciplined party. The party tolerated within its ranks a diversity of views and never tried to impose a uniform ideology on its members in the way that the Bolsheviks did. There were SRs who were straightforward populists, SRs who flirted with Marxism, SRs who were bloodthirsty fanatics and SRs who were comparative moderates. The diversity of opinion to be found within the SR ranks left the party vulnerable to splits and breakaways.

Socialist Revolutionary ideas

Victor Chernov was the SRs' main political theorist. In his writings he set out what might be called mainstream Socialist Revolutionary thinking.

- Chernov insisted that the SRs were a socialist party but acknowledged that its socialism was of a distinctive kind. Russia's uniqueness as a country, he argued, meant that it had to take its own 'special path' to socialism.

- Russia's uniqueness, said Chernov, lay in its vast peasant population and its distinctive peasant institutions, notably the *mir* (the village commune). He wanted Russia to remain a largely peasant society. He therefore maintained that Russian socialism had to be peasant-based and had to be built around peasant institutions. This position contrasted sharply with that of the Marxists, who saw the industrial workers, not the peasantry, as the foundation on which socialism was to be built.

- Chernov envisaged a Russia which consisted of a large number of self-governing village communities. These communities would own the land they farmed collectively. It was this belief in the communal ownership of land that made Socialist Revolutionary thinking socialist.

- Chernov did not want to see an all-powerful government dictating things from above. A belief in the decentralisation of power was central to Socialist Revolutionary thinking. There was more than a tinge of anarchism in the mainstream Socialist Revolutionary outlook.

- The SRs were, as their name implies, a revolutionary party – that is, they were ready to use force and violence to seize political power. To many SRs, revolutionary violence was a disagreeable necessity, but others in the party were addicted to violence and embraced the use of terrorist methods.

- The key elements in the SRs' thinking were a belief in a form of peasant based socialism, support for the idea of a decentralised political system built around the *mir*, and a readiness to use violence to further their cause.

The Combat Organisation

The Combat Organisation was the terrorist wing of the SRs. Its preferred tactic was assassination. In the early 1900s it launched a series of audacious attacks on prominent members of the Tsarist regime. These attacks did little to deflect the regime from its chosen course but they gave the SRs heroic status in the eyes of the peasantry.

The leader of the Combat Organisation in the early 1900s was Evno Azef (1869–1918). Azef, the son of an impoverished Jewish family from the Baltic region, became involved in radical politics while still in his teens. In the 1890s, when in exile in Germany, he offered his services to the *Okhrana* as an informant. From then on, until he was unmasked in 1908, Azef led an extraordinary double-life as a terrorist organiser and a police spy.

Another terrorist group, not to be confused with the Combat Organisation, were the Maximalists. The Maximalists began life as a faction within the Socialist Revolutionary Party, but broke away from it in 1906. Even more ruthless and fanatical than the Combat Organisation, the Maximalists' most notorious exploit was a bomb attack in 1906 on the holiday home of P.A. Stolypin, newly-appointed Chairman of the Tsar's Council of Ministers. Stolypin survived, but 33 others were killed.

Essential notes

Socialism can be defined in general terms as a political doctrine which seeks to replace the private ownership and control of the land, industry and financial institutions with a system of public or communal ownership.

Essential notes

Anarchism is a political doctrine that is hostile to government, the state and central authority. It prizes individual freedom and voluntary cooperation between individuals at the local level.

Essential notes

Terrorism is a political strategy that seeks, through the use of targeted or random acts of violence, to intimidate governments, and to focus attention on the terrorists' cause.

Essential notes

The victims of the Combat Organisation in the early 1900s included three senior government ministers and the Governor-General of Moscow.

Continued on the next two pages

Opposition parties: Social Democrats

Marxism

Marxism is at its core a theory about history. Karl Marx believed that he had discovered the laws which govern human history. Marx called his ideas 'scientific socialism' to distinguish them from the ideas of socialists he regarded as mere dreamers or 'utopians'.

In Marx's view, history was driven forward by economic change and by the conflicts between classes arising out of economic change. Societies, he said, passed through a series of stages, each with its own economic system and its own class structure. Economic change created new classes, triggered class conflicts and brought about movement to the next stage. In his writings Marx was preoccupied with three of these historical stages: feudalism, capitalism and communism.

Marx's theory of history

Feudal stage
In a feudal society the dominant, exploiting class were the landowners: the exploited and impoverished class were the peasantry.

Transition from feudalism to capitalism
The growth of industry, Marx stated, would create new social classes – the bourgeoisie, the owners of the 'means of production' (factories, banks and so on) and the proletariat (workers with nothing to sell except their own labour). The bourgeoisie, on the basis of its fast-growing economic strength, would inevitably challenge the political dominance of feudal landowners and would seize power from them in 'bourgeois revolutions'.

Capitalist stage
In capitalist societies, said Marx, the most enterprising members of the bourgeoisie would see off their competitors and create ever-larger, monopolistic businesses. The bourgeoisie would therefore grow progressively richer and numerically smaller, while the proletariat would grow progressively poorer (because it would be ever more ruthlessly exploited by monopolists) and numerically larger (because its ranks would be swelled by failed members of the bourgeoisie).

Transition from capitalism to communism
As a result of deepening poverty – what Marxists call 'immiseration' – the proletariat, said Marx, would eventually reach breaking point and rise up in revolt against the bourgeoisie. In the end, Marx claimed, proletarian revolutions were bound to be successful because the proletariat would have numbers on its side.

Communism
Marx believed that proletarian revolutions would give rise to communist societies in which industrial production would be based on collective rather than individual ownership. He further argued that, unlike feudal and capitalist societies, communist societies would not be plagued by class conflict – because there would be only one class, the proletariat.

Formation of the Russian Social Democratic Labour Party

A Marxist party aiming at a proletarian revolution stood little chance of making an impact on politics in late Tsarist Russia. Russia was a peasant country which lacked a sizeable proletariat.

Organised Russian Marxist groups nevertheless began to make an appearance in the 1880s and 1890s. The Liberation of Labour Group was founded by political exiles, G.V. Plekhanov chief among them, in 1883. In 1895 it merged with another exile group, the Union of Russian Social Democrats Abroad. Meanwhile, in Russia, an illegal underground organisation called the Union of Struggle for the Emancipation of the Working Class began to organise strikes in the factories of St Petersburg. Its leaders were V.I. Lenin and Yuli Martov.

In 1898 these various bodies came together to form the Russian Social Democratic Labour Party (RSDLP). Lenin and Martov took charge and established a newspaper, *Iskra* ('The Spark'), to mobilise support for the new party in 1900.

The Bolshevik – Menshevik split

The infant RSDLP split in 1903 at the Second Congress of the Party, held in Brussels and then London. The Congress was attended by a mere 43 delegates – this indicates the insignificance of Russian Marxism in the early 1900s.

On the face of it, the 1903 split was about party membership. Lenin wanted to confine RSDLP membership to those committed to 'personal participation' in its work. Martov wanted membership to be open to anyone undertaking 'regular work' for the RSDLP or its associated organisations. Behind these rival definitions, however, lay more fundamental differences.

- Lenin wanted the RSDLP to become a party of elite professional revolutionaries operating under tight, centralised leadership. Martov favoured a broader-based, more decentralised party.

- Martov believed that proletarian revolution in Russia was a long way off. In the short term he wanted the RSDLP to concentrate on helping Russia's workers to form effective trade unions. Lenin, convinced there was a realistic prospect of a proletarian revolution in the near future, saw trade union activity as a distraction.

Lenin won the day at the 1903 Congress. His followers became known as Bolsheviks (majority) while Martov's became known as Mensheviks (minority). After 1903, Bolsheviks and Mensheviks developed as separate parties.

Leninism

Lenin was a prolific writer throughout his political career. In his pre-war writings he showed himself to be highly adept at interpreting Marxism to suit his own purposes. In *The Development of Capitalism in Russia* (1896) he maintained that Russia was a capitalist country, not a feudal one; in *What Is To Be Done?* (1902) he anticipated the split with the Mensheviks by arguing that Marxists should concentrate on preparing for revolution and not waste energy in trying to bring about social reforms; and in articles written in 1905 he suggested that Russia could make the transition from capitalism to communism within a very short space of time.

Essential notes

Lenin (1870–1924) was born Vladimir Ilyich Ulyanov, the son of a high-ranking civil servant. The pseudonym Lenin was derived from the name of the River *Lena* in Siberia, where the young Ulyanov was exiled between 1897 and 1900. Lenin was a political activist from his late teens onwards. A traumatic experience, likely to have been influential in radicalising him politically, was the execution of his older brother in 1887 for involvement in a plot to assassinate Alexander III. Lenin lived in exile between 1900 and 1917, mostly in Switzerland.

Essential notes

Yuli Martov (1873–1923), real name Tsederbaum, was the son of a Jewish middle-class family. In the years 1903–17 he orchestrated Menshevik political activity from exile abroad.

The 1905 Revolution

Preconditions and triggers of revolution

Historians have distinguished between the preconditions and triggers of revolutions.

The preconditions of revolution were certainly present in Russia in the early 1900s:

- an impoverished, land-hungry peasantry, vulnerable to crop failure and struggling to cope with the twin burden of redemption payments and heavy indirect taxes

- an urban working class, small in numbers but strategically located in Russia's major cities, wrestling with appalling living and working conditions

- an educated middle class, increasing in numbers and generally liberal in outlook, which viewed Tsarist autocracy as morally and intellectually indefensible.

That this situation had arisen was in no small part the result of the Tsarist regime's attempts to modernise Russia through industrialisation. Industrialisation unleashed forces the regime struggled to control. What Tsarist Russia experienced in the late 19th and early 20th century, says one historian, was 'a crisis of modernisation' (S.A. Smith, *The Russian Revolution: A Very Short Introduction*).

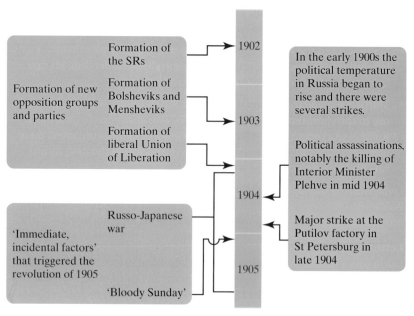

Causes of the 1905 Revolution

The Russo-Japanese War, 1904–5

Late Tsarist Russia was an expansionist power. It sought influence in south-eastern Europe at the expense of the declining Turkish Empire and in the Far East at the expense of the ramshackle Chinese Empire. The attractions of China were markets, the mineral wealth of the north Chinese province of Manchuria and a 'warm water' seaport open throughout the year (Vladivostok, Russia's main Pacific port, was iced over in winter).

Russian ambitions in the Far East were matched by those of Japan, a rising industrial and military power. In the 1890s, relations between the two countries became increasingly tense. In 1895, Russia was instrumental in thwarting Japan's hopes of making significant territorial gains after its victory in the 1894–5 Sino-Japanese war. Russia infuriated Japan further in 1898 by leasing – from China – Port Arthur, a place on which the Japanese had designs of their own. Attempts by the two countries in the early 1900s to settle their quarrel through negotiations failed.

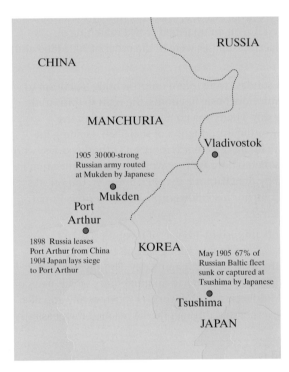

The Russo-Japanese War 1904–5

👉 **Continued on the next four pages**

Be prepared for questions asking you to consider the relative importance of the Russo-Japanese war as a cause of the 1905 Revolution. Remember, first of all, that it was a trigger rather than a precondition of revolution. Next, remember that it was not as important a trigger as 'Bloody Sunday'. The chronology of events helps to explain why. It is true that the war started before the Revolution and Russia's first major humiliation, the surrender of Port Arthur, occurred very early in 1905. However, the catastrophic defeats at Mukden (land battle) and Tsushima (naval battle) happened *after* the 1905 revolution was under way. So Mukden and Tsushima didn't trigger revolution: they just made a bad situation for Nicholas II even worse.

Russia went to war in 1904 under-prepared and over-confident. The Tsar and his advisers viewed the Japanese as racial inferiors who would be easily brushed aside. Some even believed that war would help the regime overcome its domestic problems. 'What we need to hold Russia back from revolution,' said Interior Minister Plehve in 1904, 'is a small victorious war.' In the event Russia suffered a series of humiliations:

- In 1904, Japan laid siege to Port Arthur, destroying Russia's Pacific Fleet in the process. In January 1905, Port Arthur surrendered.

- In February 1905, a 300 000-strong Russian army was routed at the battle of Mukden.

- In May 1905, after sailing about 30 000 km to do battle with the Japanese, two-thirds of the Russian Baltic fleet was sunk or captured at Tsushima.

- Under the Treaty of Portsmouth (September 1905) Russia agreed to abandon both Port Arthur and its ambitions in Manchuria.

'Bloody Sunday', January 1905

'Bloody Sunday' is the name given to the episode in January 1905 when Russian army units opened fire on an unarmed crowd marching on St Petersburg's Winter Palace. Casualties were in the order of 200 killed and 800 wounded.

The marchers on 'Bloody Sunday' were intent on presenting a petition to the Tsar calling for a constitution, basic freedoms, the right to form trade unions and an eight-hour day. There was no reference to either the abolition of the monarchy or the introduction of socialism. Leading the marchers was the shadowy figure of Father Gapon, an Orthodox priest who headed the Assembly of St Petersburg Factory Workers – an organisation at one point secretly backed by the *Okhrana*. By 1905, however, Gapon was acting on his own. Neither he nor his followers posed any serious threat to the regime.

'Bloody Sunday' was a more important 'trigger' of revolution than the Russo-Japanese war. The war was fought a long way off but 'Bloody Sunday' happened in the heart of Russia's capital city. The spectacle of peaceful demonstrators being shot down had an immediacy which news of faraway defeats did not. Middle classes and workers were equally appalled. The shock waves which reverberated through Russia reached the peasantry as well.

Russia in turmoil, 1905

Russia was in disarray in the months after 'Bloody Sunday'. Authority was defied and challenged in any number of ways.

There is no one single thread of events to follow. One way through the confusion is to consider separately the actions of the different aggrieved groups in Russian society in 1905.

Middle-class liberals	Urban working class	Peasantry	Army and navy	Non-Russian nationalities
February 1905: Congress of *zemstvo* representatives called for establishment of a democratically elected assembly to draw up new constitution.	January 1905: After 'Bloody Sunday', huge wave of strikes across the whole country. Strikes continued sporadically into spring and summer.	March 1905: Peasant disturbances broke out in 'Black Earth' region.	June 1905: Naval mutiny in the Black Sea fleet based at Sebastopol caused by harsh discipline, poor conditions and collapse of morale after Russia's humiliation in the naval battle of Tsushima (May 1905). Most committed mutineers were crew of battleship *Potemkin*.	General strike in Poland in January and February 1905 followed by demonstrations in Warsaw and Lodz in spring 1905. Violently broken up by the Russian army, with scores of people being killed. Russia kept an army of 300 000 in Poland in 1905–6 to maintain order. Strikes in Poland continued into 1906.

May 1905: All universities shut down after wave of student protest.	October 1905: Railway workers' strike paralysed the country and led to Empire-wide general strike, calling for an eight-hour day, basic rights and a constitution.	July 1905: SRs formed the Peasants' Union as a counterpart to the liberal Union of Unions.	October 1905: Localised mutinies at army barracks in St Petersburg and Moscow, mutiny at the Kronstadt naval base outside St Petersburg.	General strike in Finland in October 1905 led to demands for full self-government and concessions from Tsarist regime.

June 1905: The 'Union of Unions' formed to coordinate liberal political activity.	October 1905: St Petersburg Soviet – a council made up of elected workers' representatives – established to spearhead workers' cause: Leon Trotsky became its leading figure.	October 1905: Renewed peasant unrest, far more widespread and much more serious than earlier in the year, involving burning and looting of landowners' estates. Landowners forced to flee for their lives.		Serious unrest in Baltic provinces, especially Latvia, where army opened fire on protest march in January 1905, killing 70 people.

October 1905: Constitutional Democratic Party, known as the Kadets, founded, after legalisation of political parties; continued to oppose Tsarism. Moderate liberals saw, in the October Manifesto, a basis for compromise with the regime. Formed separate party, the Octobrists.	December 1905: St Petersburg Soviet forcibly disbanded and its leaders arrested. Armed uprising by workers in Moscow crushed.	November 1905: Leaders of Peasants' Union arrested.		Serious unrest in Georgia in south European Russia.

		Violence and disorder in countryside continued unabated into 1906.		

Events in 1905

Continued on the next two pages

Two general points should be borne in mind about the events of 1905:

- There were disturbances and disorder throughout the year, but it was in October that the Tsarist regime was in greatest danger: it was confronted simultaneously with ongoing liberal agitation, a general strike and peasant disorder on a massive scale.

- Just as the Tsarist regime struggled to control events, so too did the opposition groups and parties. Much of what happened at grass-roots level in 1905 was spontaneous. Opposition parties tried to direct protest and channel it in particular ways, but they had only limited success.

The regime's early responses

Nicholas II was a conscientious ruler, dutifully attending to matters of state, but he was also indecisive, impressionable, insensitive and intellectually under-powered. One leading historian of revolutionary Russia has called him 'something of a simpleton' (Richard Pipes, *The Russian Revolution 1899–1919*). Nicholas II was also a convinced autocrat. In 1895 he told a meeting of *zemstvo* representatives that any thoughts they had about participation in government were 'senseless dreams'.

The decision-making of Nicholas II and his advisers in 1904 to early 1905 was a catalogue of misjudgements:

- Russia's aggressive Far Eastern policy, culminating in the war against Japan, misfired completely.

- After the murder of Plehve (July 1904) Nicholas II appointed a relatively liberal Interior Minister (Prince Sviatopolk-Mirsky). This did nothing to placate Tsarism's opponents: it only made them bolder.

- Had sensible preparations been made to deal with Father Gapon's march in January 1905, the day could easily have passed off without incident.

- No coherent policy was devised in early 1905 in response to the deteriorating situation in Russia. The regime wavered between straightforward repression and half-hearted concessions, notably the promise (made in February 1905) of an elected consultative assembly.

The October Manifesto

Against the background of a shattering defeat at Tsushima, working-class militancy, peasant revolt and intensifying liberal pressure, Nicholas II turned in desperation to Witte, sidelined since 1903. Witte first negotiated the Treaty of Portsmouth to end the Russo-Japanese war (September 1905) and then, the October general strike having broken out, persuaded the Tsar to offer major political concessions. With the title of Chairman of the Council of Ministers, Witte was now effectively Russia's prime minister.

The major concessions came in the form of the October Manifesto, which promised guarantees of basic rights and the establishment of an elected law-making body (the Duma) with real power. Nicholas had, it appeared, abandoned autocracy and transformed himself into a constitutional monarch. Momentarily, the opposition was triumphant.

Aggrieved peasantry
Grievances largely economic: poverty, insecurity, 'land hunger', high taxes, redemption payments.

Discontented working class
Grievances largely economic: low wages, long hours, harsh factory discipline, poor housing.

Dissatisfied middle class
Grievances largely political: dislike of autocracy, desire for a constitution establishing representative institutions and guaranteeing basic rights.

Preconditions

Causes of the 1905 Revolution

Triggers

Russo-Japanese War, 1904–5
Exposed ineptitude of the Tsarist regime.

'Bloody Sunday', 1905
Exposed brutality of the Tsarist regime.

Causes of the 1905 Revolution: a summary

Suppression of the Soviet

The October Manifesto certainly did not bring an end to disorder in Russia. Nor were those who welcomed it as a breakthrough confident that the Tsar would keep his promises. The October Manifesto did, however, give the Tsarist regime breathing-space. The general strike was called off and liberals paused to reflect on their next move. Witte, a shrewd political operator, moved on to the offensive. When the St Petersburg Soviet, to a mixed reception from the capital's workers, called for a fresh round of strikes, Witte ordered its suppression. Trotsky, along with 250 Soviet delegates, was arrested. Soon afterwards, a Bolshevik-inspired armed uprising in Moscow was ruthlessly crushed, over 500 being killed. Witte's reward for his efforts to save Tsarism was abrupt dismissal by Nicholas II in 1906.

Why did Tsarism survive in 1905?

- After the drift and hesitation of early and mid-1905, the government, under Witte's direction, recovered its nerve and used repressive methods effectively.

- Although there were localised mutinies, the army as a whole remained loyal to the regime and obeyed orders to suppress the St Petersburg Soviet and the Moscow uprising – and, later, peasant disorder.

- Government concessions in October gave it breathing space and also split the liberal opposition to Tsarism: moderate liberals (the Octobrists) saw the October Manifesto as a basis on which to cooperate with the regime but radical liberals (the Kadets) continued to oppose it.

- The opposition parties were unable fully to control popular protest and to exploit it effectively for their own purposes.

- The various groups opposed to Tsarism – liberals, SRs, Marxists, minority nationalities – did not coordinate their efforts but pursued their own separate agendas.

- Liberals wanted to end autocracy but they were also alarmed by working-class militancy and the danger of Russia slipping into anarchy. Cooperation between middle-class and working-class opponents of Tsarism was therefore limited.

- Strikes meant financial hardship for strikers, as they lost pay. Strikes could not be sustained indefinitely. Working-class militancy ran out of steam.

Essential notes

Leon Trotsky (1879–1940), real name Lev Davidovich Bronstein, was born into a Jewish landowning family in the Ukraine. He became a member of the RSDLP in 1902, but after the split of 1903 sided with neither the Bolsheviks nor the Mensheviks, preferring to play a lone hand. A charismatic figure, Trotsky was chairman of the St Petersburg Soviet during its six-week existence (October–November 1905).

Examiners' notes

In the examination you could be asked to weigh the relative importance of the reasons why Tsarism survived the 1905 Revolution – for example, 'The main reason why Tsarism survived the 1905 Revolution was divisions among its opponents: how far do you agree?' Other factors which would need to be considered in a response to this particular question would include the regime's concessions, the impact of repression and the retention of army support.

Repression in rural Russia in and after 1905

The year 1905 was the most turbulent in a period of disorder in Russia, which lasted from 1904 until 1907. By the end of 1905 order had been largely restored in Russia's urban centres. The same was not true of the countryside, which remained out of control. In 1906, for example, terrorist attacks, most of which took place in rural areas, left 1600 government officials killed or wounded. The need to bring peasant Russia to heel was at this point the most urgent task facing the Tsarist regime.

Repression in the countryside before Stolypin

The regime's attempts to pacify the countryside began in late 1905, under Interior Minister P.N. Durnovo. Army units were sent into the main areas of peasant revolt with orders to be merciless. Over the next six months a wave of killings, beatings and arrests left an estimated 15 000 dead, 20 000 wounded and 45 000 exiled. In some cases whole villages were burned to the ground. The object of this exercise was not just to punish wrongdoers but also to intimidate the mass of the rural population into submission. It amounted to a policy of state terrorism.

Stolypin and repression in the countryside

In May 1906, Durnovo was replaced at the Interior Ministry by P.A. Stolypin. Soon afterwards (July 1906), Stolypin became Chairman of the Council of Ministers, a post he held in conjunction with that of Interior Minister until his assassination in 1911. Stolypin owed his meteoric rise to his effectiveness as governor of Saratov, in 1905 one of the most unruly provinces in southern Russia.

Repression in the countryside under Stolypin was as savage as it had been under Durnovo. In August 1906 Stolypin declared a state of emergency covering virtually the whole of rural Russia. At the same time, he introduced arrangements which allowed courts composed of five army officers to try to punish peasants accused of disorder, outside the ordinary framework of the law. Stolypin's courts-martial had a number of distinctive features.

- Cases were heard within 24 hours of the offence being committed.
- Trials were held in secret.
- The accused did not have the right to be represented by a lawyer.
- Trials lasted for a maximum of two days.
- Death sentences were carried out within 24 hours of the court reaching its decision.
- No appeals against verdicts or sentences were allowed.

In 1906–7, over 1000 people were sentenced to death under these procedures. Thousands more were sentenced to exile in Siberia. The hangman's noose became known in Russia as 'Stolypin's necktie' and the trains carrying off those exiled as 'Stolypin's wagons'.

Essential notes

P.A. Stolypin (1862–1911) belonged to an old-established Russian noble family. Stolypin was intelligent, physically courageous, strong-willed and arrogant.

The Black Hundreds

In 1905 the Tsarist regime retained the support of a significant minority of Russia's population. Some of these supporters (army officers, civil servants, senior policemen, Russian Orthodox priests) were part of the machinery of the state but others (landowners, financiers, major industrialists) were not. These people shared a belief in 'Orthodoxy, Autocracy and Nationality', and a hatred of those they regarded as subversives – notably Poles, Jews and the intelligentsia.

In 1905 Tsarism's supporters were not passive onlookers but sprang to the regime's defence. Some of the Black Hundreds' activities were lawful – holding demonstrations, for example – but they were also quick to resort to illegality and violence. In particular, they were heavily involved in organising pogroms – orchestrated attacks – on Jews and Jewish property. The Black Hundreds targeted Jews for two reasons:

- As extreme anti-Semitic conservatives, they were convinced that the Empire's Jews were plotting its downfall.

- They hoped that blaming Jews for Russia's problems would deflect attention away from the Tsar.

In 1905–6 there were nearly 700 separate attacks on Jewish communities in Russia. The worst took place at Odessa on the Black Sea in late 1905: more than 400 Jews were killed.

The Black Hundreds were not simply front organisations, or puppets, of the Tsarist regime. There were government ministers, Witte especially, who wanted nothing to do with them and who condemned their activities. There were, however, links between the regime and the Black Hundreds. The Interior Ministry supported some Black Hundreds financially and at the local level some police chiefs were involved in organising Black Hundred violence. Because Black Hundred thuggery was to some extent state-sponsored, it can be seen as an element in the regime's strategy in and after 1905 to overcome its enemies.

Conclusion

Peasant disorder did not subside quickly or completely after 1905–6. Serious disturbances continued into 1907 and beyond. Essentially, though, the violence unleashed by the state directly (through the army) or indirectly (through the Black Hundreds) did its work. The regime successfully reasserted its authority in the countryside.

Essential notes

The Black Hundreds were pro-Tsarist, anti-revolutionary groups who supported Tsarist autocracy against enemies of the regime, such as Jews and the intelligentsia. They staged raids and violent attacks against their enemies.

Essential notes

'Orthodoxy, Autocracy, Nationality' was a slogan coined by S.S. Uvarov, one of Nicholas I's ministers, in the early 19th century. It summed up the outlook of Tsarism's most committed supporters – a devotion to Orthodox Christianity, unconditional loyalty to the Romanov dynasty and intense patriotism.

Essential notes

The Black Hundreds hated Witte and rejoiced in his downfall in 1906. They held him responsible for the October Manifesto, which they saw as a betrayal of the principle of autocracy and, as anti-Semites, found it hard to overlook his wife's Jewish background.

Reform and its impact, 1906–14

The implementation of the October Manifesto

The 1905 October Manifesto was barely 350 words long. It was a statement of broad intent, not a detailed programme for reform. Only in April 1906 did the regime publish its detailed plans for a new political structure – the Fundamental Laws. Much had changed in the six-month gap between the publication of the October Manifesto and the announcement of the Fundamental Laws. Public order had to a large extent been restored and the regime was back in control. Nicholas II felt able to backtrack on the concessions he had been forced to make in October 1905. An early indication of the government's intentions was given in late 1905 when arrangements for electing the Duma were made known. The Fundamental Laws made it clear that the powers of the Duma were to be severely restricted. The provisions of the Fundamental Laws fell a long way short of what liberals and others had expected and left them feeling cheated and betrayed.

- Article 4 of the Fundamental Law declared that 'Supreme Autocratic Power belongs to the Tsar' – a description which suggested that the power of the Tsar was unchanged.

- Important areas of government policy, such as defence and foreign affairs, were declared to be the preserve of the Tsar alone.

- The Tsar was given the power to dissolve the Duma at any time of his choosing.

- Under the Fundamental Law the Tsar appointed his own ministers and advisers without any need for Duma approval.

- Article 87 of the Fundamental Law gave the Tsar the right to proclaim new laws without reference to the Duma at times when it was not in session. Laws made in this fashion had to be subsequently ratified by the Duma – but ratification could be delayed until years later.

- There was no mention of a two-house – or bicameral – arrangement in the October Manifesto. The Fundamental Law, however, established a counterweight to the Duma in the shape of the Imperial State Council. This was designed to be a solidly conservative body: half of its members were appointed by the Tsar and the other half were chosen by institutions such as the nobility, the Orthodox Church and the *zemstva*. Its law-making powers were equal to those of the Duma – meaning that it could block anything the Duma did.

The four Dumas, 1906–14

Four separate Dumas sat in the period from 1906 to 1914. The first two were dominated by opponents of Tsarism and did not last long.

The first Duma (April–July 1906)
Much to the alarm of the Tsarist government, nearly three-quarters of those successful in the 1906 Duma elections were liberals, radicals or socialists. The Kadets (liberals) were the largest single party with 182 out of 448 seats.
In early sessions of the Duma, the anti-Tsarist majority called on the government to introduce far-reaching reforms (abolition of the State Council, for instance). The regime responded by dissolving the Duma after only 73 days.
Liberal Duma members meeting in Finland appealed to the Russian public to refuse to pay taxes in protest against the government's action.
The second Duma (February–June 1907)
In the second round of Duma elections, the Kadets lost ground but the various socialist parties (SRs and their allies, Marxists) made gains. Supporters of Tsarism remained in a minority.
By the time the second Duma met, Stolypin had taken over as Chairman of the Council of Ministers. Stolypin made a genuine effort to cooperate with the Duma's middle-class liberals, hoping to draw them over to the regime's side, but got nowhere. The Duma liberals refused to support Stolypin's plans for land reform. The second Duma was, like the first, dissolved.

In mid-1907, Stolypin abruptly changed the way in which the Duma was elected, making controversial and improper use of Article 87 of the Fundamental Laws. His aim was to ensure that future Dumas had a solid conservative majority. No one lost the right to vote under the new electoral law, but the number of Duma members chosen by each of the electoral 'colleges' was drastically altered. Under the revised arrangements, the nobility (under one per cent of the population) elected more than half of the Duma while the peasantry (over 80 per cent of the population) elected only one-fifth of it. The third and fourth Dumas were unrepresentative bodies brought into being by an illegal act.

The third Duma (November 1907–June 1912)
The left-wing parties (Kadets and socialists) had fewer than 100 seats between them. The third Duma was dominated by the Octobrists (154 seats) and the right-wing parties (around 150 seats).
Plans put forward by Stolypin in 1910 to establish *zemstva* in those regions which did not have them ran into strong opposition from the right-wing parties. This clash left Stolypin seriously damaged politically.
The third Duma lasted its full five-year term.
The fourth Duma (November 1912–February 1917)
The composition of the fourth Duma was similar to that of the third: the Octobrists were a little weaker than before and the right-wing parties a little stronger.
The Octobrists became more critical of the regime than previously.

☞ **Continued on the next two pages**

Stolypin's land reforms: aims and methods

Some of Nicholas II's advisers in 1905–6 believed that once the Tsarist regime had crushed its enemies by force it could carry on much as before. Stolypin disagreed. He certainly saw that repression could not by itself ensure the long-term survival of the regime: there had to be reform as well. As Russia's chief minister after 1906 he therefore set out to perform a delicate balancing act. He was not successful. His repressive measures alienated liberals and his reforms antagonised conservatives. At the time of his assassination in 1911 he was an isolated figure.

Stolypin saw land reform as the key to Tsarism's survival. He aimed to break up the village commune (or *mir*), do away with open-field strip farming and reconstruct Russian agriculture on the basis of peasants owning their own separate farms. He believed that reform along these lines would bring economic as well as political benefits.

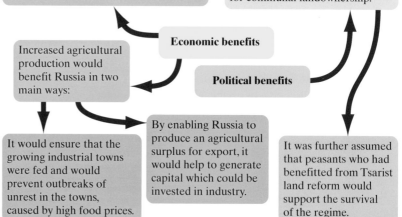

Economic and political benefits of the land reforms

In summary, the hope was that land reform would create a class of well-off, politically conservative peasant farmers. Stolypin told the Duma in 1908: 'The government has put its wager not on the drunken and the weak but on the sober and the strong – on the sturdy individual proprietor.'

The Stolypin land reform was a hugely complex affair. The key features of the measures passed during 1906–11 were as follows:

- In villages where periodic redistribution of strips had been practised after 1861 (so-called 'repartitional communes'), separate small farms could only be created after a vote among villagers.

- Every peasant householder could demand that their share of communal land be turned into their private property.

- In villages where there had been no redistribution of strips since emancipation in 1861 ('hereditary communes'), a peasant householder could request that their strips be converted into a separate small farm. If the commune was unwilling to grant this request it had to pay him compensation.

- The government set up local bodies called land organisation commissions to settle any disputes arising out of its land reform measures.

- The rules governing the operation of the Peasants' Land Bank, founded in 1882, were relaxed to allow enterprising peasants to borrow money at favourable interest rates to acquire more land.

Stolypin's land reforms: impact

- There was an initial rush to take advantage of the opportunities offered by Stolypin's land reforms, but this soon declined.

- By 1914 only 20 per cent or so of peasant householders had left the commune and become legal owners of the land they farmed. Not all of those who left, however, became proprietors of separate farms: around half of them owned their land in the form of strips in open fields and so still had links with the commune. In 1914 therefore, only 10 per cent or so of peasant householders were owners of separate farms. About 80 per cent remained full members of village communes.

- There was a sharp increase in agricultural production in Russia in the years before 1914, but it was not attributable simply to land reform. Other factors – a run of good harvests between 1909 and 1913, steps towards the opening up of Siberia and greater (though still relatively limited) use of machinery and fertilisers – were at least equally as important.

The implementation of Stolypin's land reforms was overtaken by war and revolution. It is therefore hard to make a judgement on their effectiveness. Their impact before 1914 was, however, relatively limited. Peasant life and peasant attitudes were not transformed.

Stolypin himself, of course, was denied any chance to refine his plans. He was shot and killed in 1911 while attending the Kiev opera. It is conceivable that figures within the Tsarist regime were implicated in his murder.

Examiners' notes

Some of the questions historians (and examiners) ask about Russia between 1881 and 1914 relate to episodes within the period – such as the 1905 Revolution – but others relate to the period as a whole: Did Russia undergo an economic transformation in these years? Did any meaningful political change take place in late Tsarist Russia? Why did the opposition to Tsarism fail?

Essential notes

This was Lenin's verdict on economic progress in Russia, made in 1911: 'In the half-century following the emancipation of the peasants the consumption of iron in Russia has increased five-fold; yet Russia remains an incredibly and unprecedentedly backward country, poverty-stricken and semi-barbaric.'

Continuity and change in Russia, 1881–1914

1881–1914: an economic transformation?

The balance diagram below points to two main conclusions about Russia's economy in the years 1881–1914:

- Late Tsarist Russia had a dual economy – a small but fast-growing industrial sector and a large but stagnant agricultural sector.

- Russia made significant economic progress in 1881–1914 but it did not experience an economic transformation.

Problems

In 1914 Russian industry was still heavily reliant on foreign capital, imported technology and government contracts.

Progress

Russian economy grew quickly by international standards between 1881 and 1914. Its average rate of growth each year was 3.5% (the UK figure was 1%).

Russia's coal, steel and iron production in 1914 still lagged far behind that of USA, Germany and UK.

In 1914 Russia was the world's fifth largest industrial power.

Unlocking of Siberia's economic potential had hardly begun.

Russia's industrial sector in 1914 was very small: only 1.4% of the population were industrial workers.

Some progress in agriculture: grain production increased by an average of 2% each year 1881–1913.

Russia's huge agricultural sector remained backward and unproductive: in 1914 about 90% of the peasantry still engaged in strip farming.

Progress and problems

1881–1914: meaningful political change?

- In 1881 Russia was a fully autocratic country and a repressive police state. In 1914 it was a largely, but not fully, autocratic country and it remained a repressive police state. The amount of meaningful political change which took place in late Tsarist Russia was therefore limited.

- Russia remained a largely autocratic country in 1914 despite the October Manifesto. Nicholas II's promise to create a Duma with real power was not honoured. The Fundamental Law of 1906 and Stolypin's revised electoral law of 1907 reduced the Duma to docility and near-impotence.

- The Duma after 1907 had nothing like the powers associated with a parliament of the British type. It could not remove from office a government which had lost the confidence of Duma members and it could not force government ministers to account for their actions on a regular basis. In practice, its consent was not even required before new laws came into operation, because the Tsar's ministers used Article 87 of the Fundamental Law to by-pass it. Article 87 empowered the government to introduce laws and seek Duma approval for them much later: Stolypin's 1906 land reform and his 1907 revised electoral law were both introduced using this procedure.

There was, however, some change – however limited – as a result of the 1905 revolution.

- Russia had a constitution of sorts in the shape of the 1906 Fundamental Law.
- The Duma may have been a talking shop, but before 1905 there was no elected representative body of any kind at the national level.
- Political parties were legalised in 1905 and within limits were free to criticise the regime. A British historian writing in the 1950s described Russia's political system after 1907 as 'a demi-semi-constitutional monarchy' (Richard Charques, *The Twilight of Imperial Russia*).

Why did the opposition to Tsarism fail?

Examination candidates are sometimes quick to suggest that the inability of Tsarism's opponents to work together was the main reason for their failure. The divisions that existed within the opposition certainly undermined its effectiveness. Broadly speaking, these divisions were of two kinds:

- Divisions between liberals and socialists – that is, divisions between people with fundamentally different political outlook. Liberals and socialists had no shared vision of the future and disagreed about the use of force.
- Divisions between people of not dissimilar political outlooks – these included Kadets and Octobrists, Bolsheviks and Mensheviks, moderate and terrorist Socialist Revolutionaries.

Inability to cooperate was not, however, the only weakness of Tsarism's opponents. The opposition parties were not mass-membership organisations with deep roots in Russian society. Nor were they always effectively led. Lenin and Chernov, for instance, were in Russia in 1905 but were unable to seize control of events. Only Trotsky had a real impact in 1905.

Another reason for the opposition's failure was the tenacity and ruthlessness with which the Tsarist regime fought for survival.

- Repression was brutal and effective. Here the roles of the *Okhrana* (throughout the period) and the army (especially in 1905–7) were crucial.
- Nicholas II may himself have been an inept, even pathetic, figure but in Witte and Stolypin he had shrewd, tough and unscrupulous ministers. At key moments, above all in October 1905, he listened to their advice.

Essential notes

A well-known verdict on the opposition to Tsarism was made in a memorandum written for the Tsar in early 1914 by the former Interior Minister P.N. Durnovo: 'The opponents of the government have no popular support. The Russian opposition is intellectual throughout, and this is its weakness, because between the intelligentsia and the people there is a profound gulf of mutual misunderstanding and distrust.'

Examiners' notes

Be prepared for examination questions which identify one cause of the failure of the opposition to Tsarism and ask you to consider its importance in relation to other causes – for example, 'How far do you agree that the use of repression was the main reason for the weakness of the opposition to Tsarism in the years 1881–1914?' or 'How far were divisions among its opponents the main reason for the survival of Tsarism in the years 1881–1914?'

Essential notes

Alexander Guchkov
(1862–1936), the
Octobrist leader, was a
Moscow industrialist.

Paul Milyukov (1859–1943),
the Kadet leader, was a history
professor at Moscow University
before entering politics.

Essential notes

Alexander Guchkov
(1862–1936), the
Octobrist leader, was a
Moscow industrialist.

Paul Milyukov (1859–1943),
the Kadet leader, was a history
professor at Moscow University
before entering politics.

Essential notes

St Petersburg was renamed
Petrograd in 1914 because it
sounded too German.

Essential notes

'A narrow-minded, reactionary,
hysterical woman and an
ignorant, weird peasant had
the destinies of an empire in
their hands.

*Nicholas Riasanovsky, A History
of Russia*

Essential notes

Tsarina Alexandra
(1872–1918) was:

- an ultra-conservative who
  consistently advised her
  impressionable husband
  against making concessions
  to liberals and radicals
- unshakably devoted to
  Rasputin because she
  believed that he alone
  could control her son's
  haemophilia (a medical
  condition in which the blood
  does not clot properly)
- deeply unpopular in
  wartime Petrograd
  on account of her
  German origins

The impact of war, 1914–7

The middle class and the war

Russia's middle class and its political parties, Guchkov's Octobrists and Milyukov's Kadets, were deeply patriotic. When war broke out in 1914 they rallied behind the government and looked forward to the destruction of Germany's armies. By 1917 they were in despair.

There were two main reasons for the change in mood: military defeat and mismanagement.

Military defeat

In 1914 Russia's generals hoped that its army, modernised and re-armed after the Russo–Japanese war, would advance into Germany and sweep all before it by sheer weight of numbers. These hopes were soon dashed. In the autumn of that year Germany halted Russia's advance at the battles of Tannenberg and the Masurian Lakes. Germany went on the offensive, conquering the whole of Russian Poland. A major Russian counter-attack in 1916, the 'Brusilov offensive', ran out of steam after a promising start. By early 1917 Russia was contemplating huge losses with nothing to show for them.

Mismanagement of the war effort

In peacetime Russia's bureaucracy had been seriously inefficient. In wartime it was overwhelmed by the demands made on it. Matters were made worse by the absence of clear leadership.

In 1915 Nicholas II, stung by Russia's early defeats, assumed personal command of Russia's armed forces. He left Petrograd for military headquarters at Mogilev, close to the front line. Day-to-day control of affairs in Petrograd passed to the Tsar's wife, Alexandra, and Rasputin. While Rasputin was in the ascendant, jobs in the government changed hands with bewildering frequency. During 1915–6 there were five different Interior Ministers, three different War Ministers and four different Agriculture Ministers. People at the time used the phrase 'ministerial leapfrog' to describe what was going on. Rasputin was murdered in 1916, but by then the damage had been done.

Even the conservative Duma turned against the Tsar. In 1915, 300 of its 430 members formed the 'Progressive Bloc' to demand 'a decisive change in methods of government'. By late 1916, leading figures in the 'Progressive Bloc' were plotting to force Nicholas II to abdicate.

The peasantry and the war

The war brought misery and increased hardship to peasant households.

- The peasantry bore most of the human cost of the war. Between 1914 and 1917 nearly 15 million men served in the Russian army. 1.8 million were killed and over 5 million were wounded or taken prisoner. The vast majority of these casualties were peasant conscripts.

- The loss of able-bodied men to the army meant that much of the farm work had to be done by women, young children and the elderly.

- The villages were hit by wartime inflation. Consumer goods such as boots and clothing became scarce and expensive after 1914.

- In 1916 the novelist Ivan Bunin, who knew peasant Russia very well, wrote: 'The people are tired of the war. They grow more furious every day.'

The working classes and the war

The urban working classes felt the impact of war most sharply through inflation. The main driver of inflation in wartime Russia was the price of food. After 1914 the supply of food to Russia's towns and cities failed to keep pace with demand, and prices rose alarmingly as a result. There were a number of reasons why food was in short supply:

- Grain production fell in wartime, mainly because some important food-producing areas were occupied by the Germans.

- There was a good deal of hoarding of grain by the peasantry. In normal circumstances peasants sold surplus grain in order to buy consumer goods. In wartime, unwilling to buy over-priced consumer goods, peasant households held on to their grain instead.

- Probably the most important reason for food shortages in the cities, however, was the inadequacy of Russia's transport system. Railway administrators understandably gave priority to military traffic but, as a result, food supplies intended for the towns were frequently left to rot in sidings.

	1914	1917
Monthly wage (unskilled worker)	20	50
Monthly wage (skilled worker)	40	80
Bag of potatoes	1	7
Bag of flour (16 kilograms)	3	16
Pair of boots	6	30

Wages and prices in Petrograd, 1914 and 1917 (in roubles)

Rampant inflation unsurprisingly gave rise to labour unrest. Strikes became an increasingly serious problem as the war went on. In 1916, three-quarters of a million working days were lost as a result of strike action in Petrograd alone – quadruple the figure for 1915. As well as strikes, Petrograd began to see workers' demonstrations, in which calls were made for an end to the war and the removal of the Tsar. Petrograd's working-class women, worn down by caring for hungry children and by spending hours queuing for bread, featured prominently in these protests. Petrograd's mothers, observed an *Okhrana* report in early 1917, were 'stockpiles of flammable material, needing only a spark to set them on fire'.

Essential notes

Grigory Rasputin (1872–1916) was the son of a Siberian peasant family who – though holding no official position in any church – became known as a *starets* ('holy man') and a healer. He was closely associated with the royal family from 1906 onwards. Rasputin was a disreputable figure on account of his allegedly debauched private life and his links with shady financiers.

Essential notes

Inflation describes a state of affairs in which prices are rising and the purchasing power of money is falling.

The February/March Revolution, 1917: the downfall of the Romanovs

The February/March Revolution

The 'February Revolution' occurred over a period of ten days and culminated with the abdication of Nicholas II.

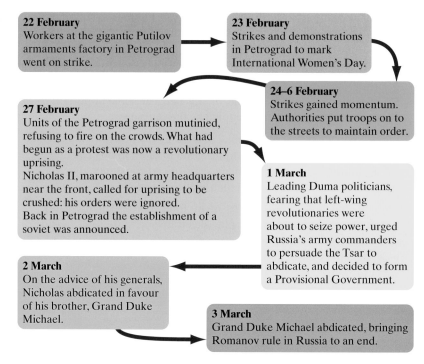

22 February
Workers at the gigantic Putilov armaments factory in Petrograd went on strike.

23 February
Strikes and demonstrations in Petrograd to mark International Women's Day.

24–6 February
Strikes gained momentum. Authorities put troops on to the streets to maintain order.

27 February
Units of the Petrograd garrison mutinied, refusing to fire on the crowds. What had begun as a protest was now a revolutionary uprising.
Nicholas II, marooned at army headquarters near the front, called for uprising to be crushed: his orders were ignored.
Back in Petrograd the establishment of a soviet was announced.

1 March
Leading Duma politicians, fearing that left-wing revolutionaries were about to seize power, urged Russia's army commanders to persuade the Tsar to abdicate, and decided to form a Provisional Government.

2 March
On the advice of his generals, Nicholas abdicated in favour of his brother, Grand Duke Michael.

3 March
Grand Duke Michael abdicated, bringing Romanov rule in Russia to an end.

The February/March Revolution

Why did Tsarism survive in 1905 but not in 1917?

The preconditions of revolution were present in much the same form in both 1905 and 1917. Throughout these years, the intelligentsia were frustrated, the peasantry impoverished and the urban working class exploited and volatile. The concessions made by the regime did little to change attitudes.

The 1906 Fundamental Laws were not seen by the liberal middle classes as an adequate response to their demands for constitutional change; the scrapping of redemption payments (1907) and Stolypin's land reform did not bring prosperity to the countryside and the legalisation of trade unions (1905) was, in the larger scheme of things, only a minor gain for the urban working class. The explanation for the different outcomes in 1905 and 1917 is not to be found in changes in the preconditions of revolution but in shorter-term, more immediate factors.

Loss of key supporters

An important difference between 1905 and 1917 was the outlook of elite institutions and groups such as the army, the bureaucracy and the industrialists. In 1905 these groups were solidly behind Tsarism; in 1917 they were not. In 1917 the Progressive Bloc in the conservative Duma wanted Nicolas II to go; his ministers deserted him in the February crisis and army generals made no move to save him.

Increased anti-government feeling

Anti-government feeling among the mass of the population – the middle class, the peasantry and the working class – was more intense in 1917 than it had been in 1905. There was no shortage of anger in Russian society in 1905 but in 1917, because of the war, it reached new levels.

In 1905 the middle class saw the Tsar as a barrier to political reform; in 1917 they saw him as an obstacle to military victory as well. Peasants were impoverished in 1905, but in 1917 they were often bereaved as well.

Wartime inflation ensured that working-class living standards were lower in 1917 than they had been in 1905.

The Provisional Government

The February Revolution was a spontaneous affair, not one masterminded by political leaders. Its success created a political vacuum. Into this vacuum moved two bodies: the Provisional Government and the Petrograd Soviet.

The Provisional Government (formed in March 1917) consisted largely of Kadets and Octobrists. At its head was Prince Lvov, a respected but uncharismatic landowner. Lvov, though, was head of the government in name only. Its leading figure was the hard-working but unimaginative Kadet leader Milyukov, who became Foreign Minister. Also influential was Guchkov, the Octobrist leader, appointed Minister of War and the Navy. The only radical in the Provisional Government was Alexander Kerensky.

The Provisional Government was a self-appointed body. Its claim to govern rested solely on the Duma background of its members. No one, however, expected that it would govern for long. It was generally accepted that its role was to be a caretaker government, administering the country's affairs while preparations were made to draw up a constitution for Russia.

The Petrograd Soviet

The Petrograd Soviet was a revival of the 1905 St Petersburg Soviet. The 1917 Soviet, however, differed from its predecessor in that it contained delegates from Petrograd's army garrison as well as from its factories: it was a council of workers' and soldiers' representatives.

The Petrograd Soviet had some 3000 members. How long any member served on the Soviet was a matter for the army unit or factory he represented. The membership of the Petrograd Soviet fluctuated and its political complexion was unpredictable. Initially it was dominated by Mensheviks and SRs, but that was to change.

Soviets sprang up in towns and cities all over Russia in 1917. By October there were about 900 of them. The Petrograd Soviet, though, was more important than any of the others. What happened in Petrograd shaped events elsewhere.

Essential notes

Before the war Alexander Kerensky (1881–1970) practised as a lawyer in Petrograd and was politically active in the Trudovik group, allies of the SRs. In 1917 he was appointed Minister of Justice at Milyukov's instigation. Aware of Kerensky's popularity among Petrograd's factory workers, Milyukov thought he would be a useful link between the Provisional Government and the Petrograd Soviet. Kerensky was a brilliant orator but was vain and impulsive.

Examiners' notes

The examination Specification divides the content of Russia in Revolution 1881–1924 into four 'bullet points' (Challenges to the Tsarist state, 1881–1906; Tsarism's last chance, 1906–17; February to October 1917; Holding on to and consolidating power, 1918–24). Remember that questions may be asked either on content to be found within the bullet points or on issues that cross bullet points. 'Why did Tsarism survive in 1905 but not in 1917?' is a good example of a question on an issue that crosses bullet points. Don't regard the four bullet points as separate, self-contained topics: the links between them need thinking about too.

The Provisional Government and its problems

Relations between the Provisional Government and the Petrograd Soviet

The Provisional Government and Petrograd Soviet differed sharply in membership and outlook.

Provisional Government	Petrograd Soviet
Membership largely liberal.	Membership socialist.
Principal supporters: middle classes, industrialists and landowners (who wanted protection from worker and peasant demands for radical economic change).	Principal supporters: Petrograd factory workers and the soldiers of the Petrograd garrison.
Welcomed the removal of the Tsar because it would enable the war to be waged more effectively.	Welcomed the removal of the Tsar because it would enable the war to be brought to an end.

A further difference between the Petrograd Soviet and the Provisional Government lay in the amount of raw power each had. Here the Soviet had the upper hand. Its support among soldiers and trade unionists gave it control of the capital's transport and communications systems. The Provisional Government, by contrast, lacked the means to force others to obey its orders.

Despite its position of strength, in the weeks following the Tsar's abdication the Petrograd Soviet was content to allow the Provisional Government to make the running. There were a number of reasons, ideological and practical, why the Mensheviks and the SRs who dominated the Petrograd Soviet were unwilling to seize control themselves.

- The Mensheviks were orthodox Marxists. They believed early 20th century Russia to be making the transition from feudalism to capitalism: the transition from capitalism to communism via a proletarian revolution seemed to be a long way off. Their instinct was therefore to watch and wait and not to make a futile bid for power.

- Conscious of their lack of administrative experience, Mensheviks and SRs believed themselves to be unqualified to govern.

- There were fears that the response of Russia's army commanders to the formation of a socialist-led government would be to try to seize power themselves, plunging the country into civil war.

The April Crisis

The Menshevik–SR abstention from power did not last long. In April 1917 the Provisional Government and the Petrograd Soviet clashed over the issue of the war.

The Kadets and Octobrists were nationalists who wanted to wage war against Germany and Austria until victory had been won. The Mensheviks and the SRs, however, were lukewarm in their attitude to the war. They were willing to fight defensively while negotiating a peace agreement with

Russia's enemies, but nothing more. This policy, known as 'revolutionary defensism', was set out in the Petrograd Soviet's 'Appeal to All the Peoples of the World' in March 1917. The Provisional Government was not prepared to embrace 'revolutionary defensism'. Its position became publicly known in April when it was revealed that Foreign Minister Milyukov had secretly informed Britain and France that Russia would fight on until victory had been achieved and would honour all the treaties made by the previous Tsarist regime. This news triggered mass demonstrations on the streets of Petrograd. Milyukov and War Minister Guchkov were forced to resign.

The April Crisis led to the reconstruction of the Provisional Government. Into government came Irakli Tsereteli, the ablest of the Mensheviks, and the SR leader Victor Chernov. Kerensky took over as War Minister. Prince Lvov remained in place as figurehead Prime Minister.

The April Crisis was significant for two main reasons:

- It brought to an end the period of uneasy co-existence between the Provisional Government's liberals and Petrograd Soviet's socialists – the period of what Lenin called 'dual power'. The leading figures of the Petrograd Soviet now dominated the Provisional Government as well.

- It effectively consigned middle-class liberals to the margins of Russian politics.

Problems facing the Provisional Government, spring 1917

The reconstructed Provisional Government faced three main problems when it took office:

- It had to decide how to provide Russia with a new constitution and a properly representative government. There was agreement among government ministers on the way forward (see below), but there were serious practical difficulties to be overcome (in particular, choice of electoral system, voting arrangements for soldiers on active service and procedures for registering voters).

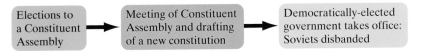

Provisional Government plans for Russia's political future

- It faced the problem of how to respond to the growing demand in Russia for peace. The April Crisis had demonstrated just how sensitive an issue this was. Anti-war feeling was strong in Petrograd and in the countryside and, not least, among soldiers serving at the front.

- It also had to contend with the problem of land seizures in rural areas. Land-hungry Russian peasants had for a long time looked enviously in the direction of privately-owned estates in their localities. In the spring of 1917, aware of events in Petrograd and sensing there was no reason to fear large-scale government-ordered reprisals, they began to seize control of landowners' estates by force. In a parallel development, peasants who had taken advantage of Stolypin's land reform to leave the village commune were pressured by their fellow villagers into rejoining it.

Essential notes

Brought up, like Stalin, in Georgia, Irakli Tsereteli (1881–1960) was a member of the second Duma in 1907. He was subsequently imprisoned and exiled by the Tsarist authorities, returning to Petrograd in March 1917.

Examiners' notes

Remember, when considering the fate of Russia's liberals just how much their strong pro-war attitude put them on the wrong side of public opinion. Apart from anti-war feeling in the towns and villages in early 1917, soldiers at the battle front were becoming massively discontented. Desertion rates rocketed: the number who deserted between the February and October Revolutions has been estimated at one million.

Lenin and the April Theses

Lenin's return to Russia

Bolshevik political activity in Petrograd in 1917 began while Lenin was still in exile abroad. Command was assumed by L.B. Kamenev. Kamenev's analysis of the situation in spring 1917 was identical with that of the Mensheviks – namely that Russia's working class was too small to take and hold on to power. Kamenev favoured supporting the Provisional Government and collaborating with the Mensheviks.

When Lenin arrived back in Petrograd in April 1917, he demanded a turnaround in Bolshevik policy.

- He called for outright opposition to the Provisional Government.

- He dismissed any idea of collaboration with the Mensheviks.

- He insisted that the Bolsheviks should launch a bid for power within a matter of months.

Kamenev and other Bolsheviks were astonished. Not only were they shocked by Lenin's readiness to ignore Marxist theory – which suggested that the transition from feudalism to capitalism to communism would be a lengthy process – but also thought he was out of touch with the mood of the Russian people.

There followed a brief period of in-fighting among the Bolsheviks, which ended with Lenin getting his way. His success was largely based on his strength of personality but it also owed something to support from new entrants into the Bolshevik ranks. These new Bolsheviks, radical in outlook and mostly working-class in origin, preferred Lenin's daring to the caution of his lieutenants.

Lenin's Bolshevik lieutenants, 1917

L.B. Kamenev, Grigory Zinoviev and Leon Trotsky were the most influential of Lenin's lieutenants.

Lenin's Bolshevik lieutenants

Kamenev 1883–1936	Zinoviev 1883–1936	Stalin 1879–1953	Trotsky 1879–1940
The son of a railway engineer, he had more humane instincts than most other leading Bolsheviks but did not always act upon them.	Born into a family of small-scale landowners, he was a persuasive public speaker but prone to lose his nerve under pressure.	A Georgian of peasant origins, he was seen by other leading Bolsheviks as a competent administrator but intellectually second-rate.	Born into a landowning family, he was able, dynamic and charismatic but also aloof, impatient and arrogant.

The April Theses

Lenin now set out to build a platform from which the Bolsheviks could launch a bid for power. The immediate need was to drum up support.

Lenin's chosen tactic was to exploit the growing unpopularity of the Provisional Government among workers, peasants and soldiers. The source of the Provisional Government's difficulties was its policies on the war, land seizures and, to a lesser extent, constitutional issues. Lenin condemned these policies and set out Bolshevik alternatives to them in the 'April Theses'. The 'April Theses' were expressed in the language of socialist principle but the policies put forward in them were highly opportunistic.

Peace

The Provisional Government was sincere in its desire for peace but what it aimed at was an all-round peace – an agreement by all combatant countries to stop fighting. It was reluctant to make a separate peace – one in which Russia made its own arrangements with Germany and Austria – for two main reasons:

- Leaving Russia's allies, Britain and France, in the lurch was felt to be dishonourable.

- Since Germany had occupied vast tracts of Russian territory, the terms of any separate peace agreement were likely to be harsh – possibly harsh enough to trigger a military coup in Russia.

These subtleties were of little concern to most ordinary Russians. They simply wanted an end to the war. This is what Lenin promised them – an immediate separate peace.

Land

The Provisional Government was fully aware of the need for land reform. It refused, though, to sanction land seizures, insisting that land reform was a matter for a future democratically elected parliament. It maintained that land seizures involved a disorderly scramble in which land was not distributed fairly – and also believed that land seizures encouraged desertion from the army, with peasant soldiers leaving the front to get back to their villages to claim their share of whatever was going. These arguments were lost on Russia's peasants who, by mid-1917, were increasingly taking the law into their own hands. Lenin encouraged them to do so. His slogan was 'All land to the peasantry' – despite the fact that, as a socialist, he was opposed the principle of private ownership of land.

'All power to the Soviets'

The Provisional Government wanted a parliament elected by all Russians to be at the heart of the country's political system. Lenin's slogan was 'All power to the Soviets'. What he was saying was that the key institution in Russia's post-revolution political arrangements should be Soviets elected by workers and soldiers, not a democratically-elected parliament. To some this was an attractive prospect:

- Among the workers of revolutionary Petrograd, there were those who hated the middle and upper classes and who were ready to deny them political rights.

- Also, Lenin's plan offered a lifeline to members of Soviets who faced an uncertain future after the Constituent Assembly had done its work and left the Soviets with no obvious role.

Note that Lenin's dislike of what he dismissed as 'bourgeois democracy' was influenced by awareness of the fact that the Bolsheviks had no chance of winning a majority in nationwide free elections.

Essential notes

The Bolsheviks used a number of slogans in 1917 to summarise their policies. The one they used most widely was 'Peace, Bread and Land'. 'Peace' referred to their policy of an immediate separate peace and 'land' to their support for peasant land seizures. The word 'bread' was there to suggest that a Bolshevik government would bring an end to the food shortages and runaway inflation, which in early 1917 were the most important source of popular discontent in big cities such as Petrograd and Moscow.

Essential notes

Petrograd in 1917 was a hotbed of working-class militancy. Trade unions grew rapidly in size and campaigned successfully for both the eight-hour day and big wage increases (the value of which was soon wiped out by inflation). Some factories saw 'workers' control' of management activities. A 20 000-strong armed workers' militia, the 'Red Guards', came into existence to defend the revolution against its enemies.

The July Days and the Kornilov affair

Increasing Bolshevik support

Between February and April 1917 membership of the Bolshevik Party increased from 25 000 to 75 000. Following the publication of the April Theses, support for the Bolsheviks increased further, especially in Petrograd, though nationally they were still behind the SRs and Mensheviks.

In the early summer of 1917 Lenin believed he could force his way into power by bringing the Petrograd crowds out on to the streets. He therefore tried to raise the political temperature, launching a ferocious propaganda campaign against the Provisional Government and calling on soldiers and workers to defy the authority of their officers and bosses.

Russia's June offensive, 1917

Along with its allies, Russia agreed to launch a major offensive on the Eastern Front in 1917. The idea was to relieve the pressure on Britain and France on the Western Front. In June 1917 the planned offensive went ahead – despite shortages of ammunition, low army morale and war weariness among civilians. After initial successes against Austrian forces, Russia's armies were driven backwards by the Germans. Soon German troops were advancing towards Petrograd itself. The Provisional Government, deeply alarmed, responded by ordering units of the Petrograd garrison to leave the city to reinforce their hard-pressed comrades at the battle front.

The July Days

A situation now arose which was tailor-made for Lenin to exploit. The units of the Petrograd garrison ordered to the front refused to go, claiming that they had a right to stay in the city to defend the revolution against those opposed to it. Radical, pro-Bolshevik elements among Petrograd's factory workers rallied to their support. So too did sailors at the naval base at Kronstadt. In early July, 20 000 armed Kronstadt sailors arrived in Petrograd to back the mutineers. They marched on the headquarters of the Petrograd Soviet, accompanied by a throng of demonstrators.

With pro-Bolshevik crowds out on the streets, the conditions for a Bolshevik seizure of power appeared to be in place. But, at the crucial moment, Lenin hesitated. He failed to give the crowds a clear lead. The Provisional Government counter-attacked. The mutinous soldiers were disarmed. Warrants were issued for the arrest of Lenin and other leading Bolsheviks. Lenin fled to nearby Finland, where he remained until shortly before the October Revolution.

The July Days were a disaster for the Bolsheviks. They appeared to have missed their chance to seize power. The verdict on the July Days, by the American historian Richard Pipes, is 'Lenin's worst blunder'.

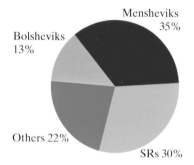

Share of the vote in the election for the first All-Russian Congress of Soviets

The Kornilov affair

The big winner in July was Kerensky. It was he who had been mainly responsible for heading off the threatened uprising. He now became Prime Minister in place of Prince Lvov who, weary of politics, stepped down.

At this point the Bolsheviks benefitted from a slice of good luck. It came in the form of General Kornilov's intervention in politics. The Kornilov affair allowed the Bolsheviks to retrieve their position.

Kornilov was appointed commander-in-chief of Russia's army by Kerensky after the July Days. He had previously been commander of the Petrograd garrison, where he had watched the events of 1917 unfold with mounting disgust. As commander-in-chief his priorities were to re-establish discipline in the army and restore order in Petrograd, thereby making it possible for Russia to fight the war effectively. He urged Kerensky to give him sweeping new powers which – had they been granted – would have made him more or less a military dictator. A series of inconclusive negotiations between Kornilov and Kerensky followed. When they finally broke down in August 1917, Kornilov ordered units of his army to advance on Petrograd.

Here, it seemed, was a counter-revolution in the making. The Petrograd Soviet's response was to mobilise its resources to defend the capital. The Bolsheviks took the lead.

- Bolshevik 'Red Guards' (armed factory workers), who had been disbanded after the July Days, were rearmed.
- Pro-Bolshevik railwaymen held up troop trains heading towards Petrograd.
- Crucially, representatives of the Petrograd Soviet, many of them Bolsheviks, infiltrated Kornilov's advancing forces and succeeded in turning the ordinary soldiers against their officers.

The advance on Petrograd petered out without a shot being fired.

Bolshevik revival

The Kornilov affair had two main political consequences.

- One was the collapse of Kerensky's reputation. His dealings with Kornilov left him vulnerable to the charge that he had taken part in a counter-revolutionary plot.
- The other was a sharp upswing in the Bolsheviks' popularity. They more than anyone, it appeared, had been responsible for the defeat of Kornilov. They were able to project themselves in their propaganda as saviours of the revolution. In September the Bolsheviks won control of the Petrograd Soviet and of soviets in a number of other major cities, Moscow among them.

Examiners' notes

Lenin is often depicted as a master political tactician, but any estimate of his abilities has to take into account his uncertainty during the July Days.

Essential notes

Lavr Kornilov (1870–1918) rose to the top of the Russian army having begun life as the son of a peasant. His background was much less privileged than Lenin's, Kerensky's or Trotsky's. A fighting general, not a deskbound administrator, Kornilov was brave and determined, but politically naive. One of his fellow-officers said of him that he had 'the heart of a lion, the brain of a sheep'. Kornilov was killed in action in one of the early battles of the Russian Civil War.

The October/November Revolution, 1917

The Bolsheviks decide on an armed uprising

In October 1917 Petrograd was effectively at the Bolsheviks' mercy. The main levers of power in the city were in their hands. These included the Military Revolutionary Committee (MRC) set up by the Petrograd Soviet after the Kornilov affair to organise forces for use against counter-revolutionaries. The question of how best to exploit the opportunity which had arisen was debated at a crucial meeting of the Bolsheviks' Central Committee on 10 October. Lenin made a flying visit to Petrograd in order to be present. He argued for an immediate seizure of power. Kamenev and Zinoviev urged caution but they were in the minority. The Committee voted 10-2 in favour of an armed uprising.

The role of Trotsky

At the tactical level the Bolshevik seizure of power was organised and directed not by Lenin but by Leon Trotsky. Trotsky planned the seizure of power with considerable skill. He aimed to give the impression that the Provisional Government was being overthrown by the soviets rather than by a small group of conspirators. His plan therefore involved seizing power in the name of the All-Russian Congress of Soviets, a body which happened to be meeting in Petrograd in late October. Since the Bolsheviks had a majority in the Congress it could be relied upon to go along with Trotsky's scheme. Trotsky also deployed the forces available to him shrewdly, giving the most important tasks to the Kronstadt sailors and Red Guards and not placing too much faith in the unreliable troops of the Petrograd garrison.

The October/November Revolution

Romanticised Bolshevik histories of the October Revolution present it as high drama, with heroic workers storming Petrograd's Winter Palace, headquarters of the Provisional Government – the first shot having been fired from the naval vessel *Aurora*, anchored nearby on the River Neva. The truth was less exciting. The Bolshevik seizure of power in Petrograd was largely uncontested.

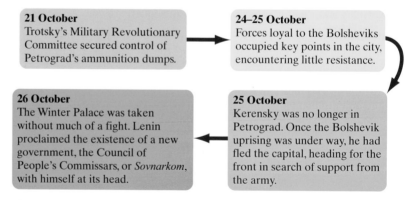

21 October
Trotsky's Military Revolutionary Committee secured control of Petrograd's ammunition dumps.

24–25 October
Forces loyal to the Bolsheviks occupied key points in the city, encountering little resistance.

26 October
The Winter Palace was taken without much of a fight. Lenin proclaimed the existence of a new government, the Council of People's Commissars, or *Sovnarkom*, with himself at its head.

25 October
Kerensky was no longer in Petrograd. Once the Bolshevik uprising was under way, he had fled the capital, heading for the front in search of support from the army.

The October/November Revolution

A parallel Bolshevik uprising took place in Moscow. Here the local Bolshevik leadership was under-prepared, and things did not go smoothly. The Bolsheviks only won control of the city after bitter fighting against forces loyal to the Provisional Government. A thousand people died in the struggle for Moscow.

The extent of Bolshevik control in Russia, October 1917

The October Revolution marked the beginning rather than the end of the Bolshevik struggle for power in Russia. In October 1917 they were only in full control of Petrograd, Moscow and a handful of other cities. In the countryside they had no real presence at all. They were also weak in the outlying areas of the Russian Empire, where separatists were quick to take advantage of the confusion at the centre: in the period from November 1917 to February 1918 there were declarations of independence in Finland, Estonia, Latvia, Lithuania, Poland and the Ukraine.

The results of the long-planned elections to the Constituent Assembly, held in late November 1917 without interference from Lenin's government, give a good indication of the extent of support for Bolshevism just after the October Revolution. Over 40 million voters took part, with only 23.7 per cent of them favouring the Bolsheviks.

	Votes (millions)	% share	Seats
SRs	17.1	41.3	380
Bolsheviks	9.8	23.7	168
Kadets	2	4.8	17
Mensheviks	1.36	3.3	18
Others	11.14	26.9	120

Constituent Assembly election results, November 1917

Why were there two revolutions in Russia in 1917?

- The February Revolution arose out of deep-rooted tensions in Russian society and was triggered by the impact of war. It swept away the Tsarist regime but left open the question of how Russia was to be governed in future.

- It was not inevitable that Russia's political future would be decided by a second revolution: it could have been decided by a democratically elected Constituent Assembly.

- The main reason why a second revolution took place was that Lenin, seeing no other route to power, was determined that it should.

- There would have been no Bolshevik revolution had the Bolsheviks remained as numerically weak as they were in February 1917. They were able to build a position of strength during 1917 for reasons that will be explored in the next chapter.

Why the Bolsheviks were able to seize power in October 1917

Factors explaining Bolshevik success

Lenin

- Without Lenin there would have been no October Revolution. Left to themselves, other Bolsheviks in early 1917 would not have launched a bid for power. All the evidence suggests they would have joined the Mensheviks in supporting the Provisional Government.

- Lenin's April Theses were the basis on which the Bolsheviks increased their support in the course of 1917. In the April Theses Lenin showed that his understanding of the mood of public opinion in Russia in 1917 was better than that of other political leaders.

- Lenin's demand for an uprising in Petrograd in the autumn of 1917 was decisive. Whether other Bolsheviks – many of whom feared they would soon be chased out of the city by counter-revolutionary forces – would have gone ahead without his urgings is doubtful.

- Lenin's conduct in 1917 was not, however, a flawless exhibition of political manoeuvring: he misjudged things badly during the July Days.

Trotsky

Trotsky's contribution to the success of the October Revolution was second only to Lenin's. His role was not confined to organising the seizure of power. He was also instrumental in winning people over to Bolshevism in mid-1917. During these months Trotsky was a more visible, high-profile figure than Lenin (who was in hiding for much of the time). He addressed meeting after meeting, becoming the idol of the revolutionary crowds in the process. One of Trotsky's biographers, Dmitri Volkogonov, calls him 'the orator-in-chief of the revolution'.

Popular support for the Bolsheviks

The October Revolution was not the work of a handful of conspirators. By late 1917 the Bolsheviks had attracted a significant amount of popular support. They may have won less than a quarter of the vote in the 1917 Constituent Assembly elections, but their position was stronger than this headline figure suggests.

- The Bolsheviks polled strongly in the major cities, especially in Petrograd and Moscow, where their share of the vote was nearly 50 per cent. In the working-class districts of these cities they won 60–70 per cent of the vote.

- Overall the Bolsheviks won about half the votes cast by members of Russia's armed forces.

Essential notes

'Had I not been present in 1917 in Petersburg, the October Revolution would still have taken place – on the condition that Lenin was present and in command. If neither Lenin nor I had been present in Petersburg, there would have been no October Revolution: the leadership of the Bolshevik Party would have prevented it from occurring – of this I have not the slightest doubt.'

Trotsky's diary, March 1935

Essential notes

The SRs split because the Right SRs wanted Russia to be governed by a democratically elected parliament while the Left SRs favoured a more radical approach in which power lay with soviets dominated by workers and peasants.

- Ballot papers used in the elections did not differentiate between the various elements of the SR party, which in late 1917 was disintegrating. The Left SRs became (temporarily, as it turned out) allies of the Bolsheviks. In late 1917, six Left SRs took up posts in *Sovnarkom*. A fair proportion of SR votes in the Constituent Assembly elections, perhaps as many as half, were cast for candidates who favoured collaboration with the Bolsheviks.

Popular support did not fall into the Bolsheviks' lap. They secured it by advancing a political programme that appealed to workers and soldiers in particular.

Weaknesses and failures of the Provisional Government
The Bolsheviks clearly benefitted from the weaknesses and failings of the Provisional Government.

- As a caretaker government, it lacked authority and legitimacy.
- Expectations of it immediately after the downfall of Nicholas II were unrealistically high: disillusionment was inevitable.
- In its early days its capacity for action was limited by the Petrograd Soviet.
- It was unable to prevent the deterioration of economic conditions in Russia in 1917, failing in particular to control runaway inflation.
- Its war and land policies were deeply unpopular.
- It could have speeded up elections to the Constituent Assembly.

Luck
The Bolsheviks were lucky in that the Kornilov affair allowed them to make a comeback after the July Days.

The October Revolution: popular uprising or coup?
The Bolsheviks claimed that the October Revolution was a popular uprising. Western historians, especially right-wing scholars such as Richard Pipes, reject this claim, arguing that the October Revolution was a *coup d'état* – the capture of power by a small minority.

Examiners' notes

The October Revolution is another topic that lends itself to questions requiring you to consider the relative importance of causes – for example, 'How important was Lenin's contribution to the success of the October Revolution?' or 'How far was the October Revolution the result of the weaknesses and failures of the Provisional Government?'

Essential notes

The failure of the Provisional Government to get things done allowed Lenin to describe its policies in mocking terms in September 1917: 'As to land, wait until the Constituent Assembly. As to the Constituent Assembly, wait until the end of the war. As to the end of the war, wait until complete victory.'

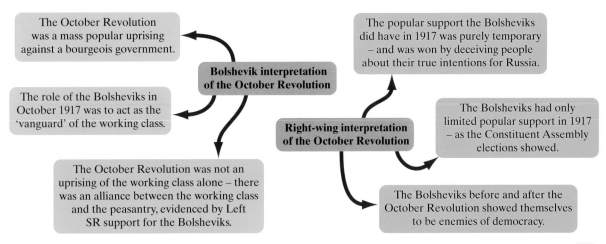

The October Revolution was a mass popular uprising against a bourgeois government.

Bolshevik interpretation of the October Revolution

The role of the Bolsheviks in October 1917 was to act as the 'vanguard' of the working class.

The October Revolution was not an uprising of the working class alone – there was an alliance between the working class and the peasantry, evidenced by Left SR support for the Bolsheviks.

The popular support the Bolsheviks did have in 1917 was purely temporary – and was won by deceiving people about their true intentions for Russia.

Right-wing interpretation of the October Revolution

The Bolsheviks had only limited popular support in 1917 – as the Constituent Assembly elections showed.

The Bolsheviks before and after the October Revolution showed themselves to be enemies of democracy.

Different interpretations of the October Revolution

The Bolsheviks in power: first steps, 1917–8

The Bolsheviks' priority after the October Revolution was to consolidate their hold on power. From the outset they were willing to use authoritarian methods. They felt that Marxist theory justified their approach.

Sovnarkom

At the time of its formation *Sovnarkom* was an all-Bolshevik body. A handful of Left SRs joined it later. Alongside Lenin as chairman, *Sovnarkom*'s members included Trotsky (Commissar for Foreign Affairs) and Stalin (Commissar for Nationalities).

Sovnarkom's first decrees in late 1917 were unashamed attempts to buy public support:

- The Decree on Peace called for an immediate cease-fire, to be followed by peace negotiations involving all combatant countries.

- The Decree on Land gave peasants the right to take over landowners' estates without compensation.

- The Workers' Decrees guaranteed a minimum wage and an eight-hour day and promised workers control in the factories.

- The 'Declaration of the Rights of the Peoples of Russia' gave national minorities the right to decide their own future, including the right to separate themselves from Russia.

Towards a one-party state

It soon became clear that the Bolsheviks would not tolerate criticism or opposition:

- Press freedom was one of the first casualties of Bolshevik rule. The Decree on the Press (October 1917) authorised the closure of all 'counter-revolutionary' newspapers – in practice, those that supported the Kadets, Mensheviks or Right SRs.

- The Kadet party was outlawed in November 1917 and its leaders arrested.

- The SRs and Mensheviks survived longer. They were barred from openly taking part in political activity in 1918, though they were able to lead a shadowy, semi-legal existence until 1921–2, when their leaders were either arrested or forced into exile.

Dissolution of the Constituent Assembly, January 1918

Lenin wrote off the Constituent Assembly in advance of its first and only meeting in January 1918.

- He claimed the make-up of the Assembly did not reflect voters' true preferences because elections had taken place before the SR split – resulting in pro-Bolshevik Left SR candidates not being clearly identified on ballot papers.

- He also asserted that 'a republic of soviets is a higher form of democracy than the usual bourgeois republic with a Constituent Assembly'.

The Constituent Assembly met for one day and was then forcibly disbanded.

The *Cheka* and the 'Red Terror'

The Bolsheviks established a political police force within weeks of seizing control in Petrograd. Its full name was the 'All-Russian Extraordinary Commission for Combating Counter-Revolution and Sabotage', or *Cheka* for short. At its head was Felix Dzerzhinsky. Initially *Cheka* activity was confined to Petrograd but within a year it was organised on a nationwide basis. By 1921 its total strength was over 150 000.

The *Cheka* was given sweeping powers of arrest, trial and execution. Accountable only to *Sovnarkom*, it was ruthless and uncompromising from the start. Things were taken to a different level, however, after the Civil War began in earnest (spring 1918), and in particular after the SR Fanya Kaplan's assassination attempt on Lenin (August 1918). The *Cheka* launched a full-scale onslaught on those sections of the population whose attitude to the Bolshevik regime was seen as hostile or uncooperative. This was known as the 'Red Terror'.

Unapologetically, *Chekists* engaged in torture, hostage-taking and mass murder. Estimates of the numbers who died at the hands of the *Cheka* throughout 1918–20 vary, but some put the figure as high as 500 000, more than were killed by the *Okhrana* under the Tsarist regime. The most prominent victims were the Tsar and his family, murdered by *Chekists* at Ekaterinburg in the Urals in July 1918.

The 1918 Constitution

In mid-1918 the Bolsheviks regularised the political arrangements made immediately after the October Revolution by incorporating them into a new constitution. The key institutions of the new state, to be named the RSFSR (Russian Socialist Federated Soviet Republic), were as shown below.

Note also that:

- those that the Bolsheviks saw as exploiters – employers, those with unearned incomes, merchants, traders and clergymen – were denied the right to vote
- the Russian Orthodox Church was separated from the state.

By mid-1918 Bolshevik Russia was a state more repressive and authoritarian than Tsarist Russia had been. Critics of Bolshevism claimed that it was by its nature dictatorial, illiberal and undemocratic. The Bolsheviks defended themselves by claiming that repressiveness had been forced on them by circumstances and would be temporary.

What is not in dispute is that the use of state terror was, from the Bolshevik point of view, effective. Additionally, since many of its victims were peasants or members of the bourgeoisie, its use did not immediately alienate the Bolsheviks' urban working-class support.

Essential notes

Born into a Polish landed gentry family, Felix Dzerzhinsky (1877–1926) was head of the *Cheka* and, after 1922, of its successor organisations, the GPU and OGPU. Lenin valued Dzerzhinsky because of his loyalty, fanaticism and administrative ability, but did not rate him highly as a political thinker or a policy-maker.

Examiners' notes

Bolshevik success in the Russian Civil War, and the reasons for it, is an important examination topic. Part of the explanation lies in the Bolsheviks' ruthlessness. This section should therefore be read in conjunction with the pages that follow.

Sovnarkom
In theory elected by and accountable to the Executive Committee. In practice the real centre of power.

Executive committee
200 strong: in theory ran things between Congresses.

All-Russian Congress of Soviets
In theory had supreme authority.

Institutions of the Russian Socialist Federated Soviet Republic

The Civil War

Reasons for the outbreak of the Civil War

The first shots in the Russian Civil War were fired in October 1917 when army units loyal to Kerensky marched on Petrograd and were sent packing by the Bolsheviks. Descent into full-scale civil war, however, came later and owed much to two developments:

- The dissolution of the Constituent Assembly by the Bolsheviks in January 1918 – to those hoping for a democratic Russia this was a step too far.

- The treaty of Brest-Litovsk (March 1918) was the last straw for the Bolsheviks' enemies because it stripped Russia of so much territory.

The treaty of Brest-Litovsk

At the time of the October Revolution the Bolsheviks hoped for an all-round peace settlement involving all the combatant countries. It soon became apparent that their hopes were unrealistic. The Bolsheviks responded by opening negotiations with Germany for a separate peace.

The price Germany demanded for peace was high: the surrender of Russian Poland, the Baltic provinces (Estonia, Latvia and Lithuania), Finland, the Ukraine and the southern Transcaucasus. These areas contained 26 per cent of Russia's population, 27 per cent of its arable land and 74 per cent of its coal and iron ore.

Many leading Bolsheviks regarded these demands as unacceptable. Lenin, however, insisted that Germany's terms had to be accepted. Three considerations shaped his thinking:

- The Bolsheviks had promised peace before the October Revolution and could not go back on their promise without alienating their supporters.

- The Russian army, seriously weakened by desertions, was losing its ability to offer any sort of resistance to the Germans.

- The Bolsheviks wanted to be able to concentrate on overcoming their internal enemies. 'The bourgeoisie has to be throttled and for that we need both hands free', said Lenin.

From the Bolshevik point of view, Brest-Litovsk solved one problem but also gave rise to new ones:

- The Left SRs, hostile to Brest-Litovsk because large tracts of peasant Russia would be lost, walked out of the coalition with Bolsheviks in protest against it.

- Russia's army commanders and its middle and upper classes, all strongly nationalistic in outlook, were outraged by what they saw as the traitorous Bolshevik surrender at Brest-Litovsk. Their aim was now to overthrow Bolshevism and continue the war.

Territory surrendered by Russia

Treaty of Brest-Litovsk, March 1918

Examiners' notes

Use simple maps, such as the one shown opposite, to help you visualise the arena in which the war took place, and the territory that was gained and lost. You do not need to know the detailed geography of the Civil War for your examination.

Continued on the next four pages

The Red Army

At the time of the October Revolution the Bolsheviks had no properly organised army. Their initial plans for an all-volunteer 'Socialist Guard' with elected commanders were scrapped, in favour of a 'Red Army' built on traditional lines.

Trotsky, principal architect of the Red Army and made Commissar for War in March 1918, appointed many ex-Tsarist officers. Some of these joined the Red Army willingly; others fought for the money; many were conscripted and prevented from deserting by the threat of reprisals against their families.

Every ex-Tsarist commander was supervised by a political commissar, or minder, who was a Bolshevik of proven loyalty.

Compulsory military service for the mass of the population was reintroduced in May 1918. Discipline in the Red Army was ferocious: deserters and those guilty of unjustified retreat were liable to be executed.

By 1921 the Red Army numbered 5.4 million but was less formidable than this figure might suggest. Many of its units were poorly trained and equipped: desertion and infectious diseases were ongoing problems.

The rival forces

The Russian Civil War was an episode of bewildering complexity. The main conflict was the one between the Bolsheviks (or Reds) and the Whites. But the Red-White conflict was only part of the story: the Bolsheviks also fought against 'Greens' and against separatist movements.

The Whites

The Bolsheviks attached the label 'Whites' to their enemies because it was a colour associated with Tsarism (the Imperial Russian Army wore white uniforms).

The Whites were political conservatives headed by former Tsarist generals and soon became the dominant force in the anti-Bolshevik camp. The Whites saw off *Komuch* in a bout of political in-fighting in late 1918 and expelled its SR leaders from Russia.

The three main White armies were the forces led by Admiral Kolchak in Siberia; the Armed Forces of Southern Russia (AFSR) commanded by General Anton Denikin and later by Baron Wrangel; and, smallest of the three, the North-Western Army headed by General Nikolai Yudenich.

The Greens

The Greens were peasant forces.

Some were linked with the SRs, for example, the 'People's Army', which fought against the Bolsheviks in Siberia in 1918. Others were freelance units concerned mainly with the defence of their own locality, notably the 15 000 strong 'Revolutionary Insurgent Army of the Ukraine' led by the anarchist Nestor Makhno (1889–1935).

Separatist movements

In 1917 the Bolsheviks promised non-Russian minorities the right to separate themselves from Russia if they wished. In practice they were not prepared to see the resources of the minority areas lost to the Bolshevik state: where breakaway regimes were set up, the Bolsheviks tried to overthrow them.

Red Army fought against, for example, Ukrainian separatist regime of Simon Petluria in 1918–20, Baltic (Estonian, Latvian and Lithuanian) separatists in 1918–19, Transcaucasian (Armenian, Georgian, and Azerbaijani) separatists in 1920–1.

The rival forces

Allied intervention

Allied troops were originally sent to Russia to support efforts to reopen an Eastern Front against Germany. The war with Germany ended in November 1918 but Allied forces were not immediately withdrawn from Russia.

Allied politicians had different reasons for wanting to remain in Russia. Some wanted to fight an ideological crusade against Bolshevism. Others were concerned with more limited objectives, such as rescuing the Czech Legion or supporting minorities struggling for independence from Russia.

Allied intervention in Russia was for the most part half-hearted. Britain was by far the most active of the interventionist powers.

The fighting, 1918–21

The areas where fighting took place are shown in the map, overleaf.

Red Army victories

- In 1918 and early 1919 the principal military threat to the Bolsheviks was posed by the Czech Legion and the forces of Admiral Kolchak, both based in the Urals region and Siberia. The Czech threat faded, but in early 1919 Kolchak's army made spectacular progress, advancing westwards and threatening Moscow (made Russia's capital in March 1918, Petrograd being considered too vulnerable to White attack). A Bolshevik counter-attack in mid-1919 then forced it on to the retreat. After further defeats in late 1919 Kolchak was captured by the Bolsheviks and executed.

- Denikin's Armed Forces of Southern Russia posed a serious threat to the Bolsheviks in late 1919, getting to within about 400 km of Moscow. They were then rolled backwards by a Bolshevik counter-attack and bottled up in the Crimean peninsula, from where they were evacuated by the Allied forces.

- Yudenich's North-Western Army came within sight of Petrograd in late 1919 before suffering defeat at the hands of a much larger Bolshevik force commanded by Trotsky.

Red Army defeats

In 1920, with the Civil War effectively over, Russia was attacked by Poland. Newly-independent Poland consisted largely of territory that Germany had taken from Russia under Brest-Litovsk and which the Allies then took from Germany. At first the Red Army did well, advancing to the gates of Warsaw, but was then driven backwards.

The Russo-Polish war was ended by the Treaty of Riga (1921) under which Russia ceded to Poland a large amount of territory on its western border.

Essential notes

The 50 000-strong Czech Legion consisted of soldiers of the Austrian army who, having been taken prisoner by the Russians, agreed to fight for them – believing that defeating Austria would bring an independent Czechoslovakia nearer. After Brest-Litovsk, the Bolsheviks arranged to send the Czechs home via Siberia. On the journey down the Trans-Siberian Railway, the Czechs became suspicious of their Bolshevik escorts, and overpowered them. Encouraged by Britain and France to fight against the Bolsheviks, the Czechs swiftly won control of most of western Siberia. After their initial success, they were weakened by mutinies and a lack of supplies and lost effectiveness.

Continued on the next two pages

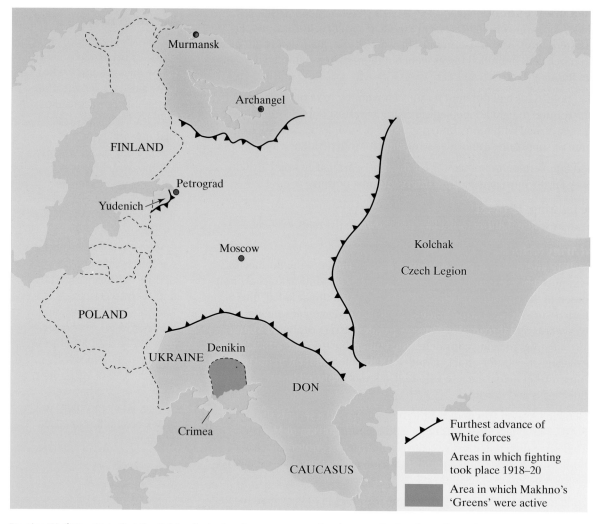

Russian Civil War. Note that the Bolsheviks had an immense strategic advantage in that throughout the war they controlled a compact heartland, with Moscow, hub of the Russian railway network, at its centre. The Whites, by contrast, were scattered around the edges of European Russia.

Problems within Bolshevik-held territory

The treaty of Brest-Litovsk and the spread of civil war deprived the Bolsheviks of large amounts of arable land, industrial plant and raw materials. As a result, Lenin's government was faced with huge economic problems in the territory it still controlled.

- Industrial output slumped.

- In the cities there were shortages of food and fuel.

- Prices soared: the value of the rouble collapsed more or less completely.

- The peasantry were unwilling to sell their produce for worthless paper money – cutting the supply of food to the cities further and driving prices even higher.

- Desperate for food, urban workers deserted the cities in massive numbers and returned to their native villages. Between 1918 and 1920 Petrograd lost three-quarters of its population. The population of Moscow halved during the same period. So, on top of all of the other difficulties, factories found themselves short of labour.

War Communism

In these desperate circumstances, the Bolsheviks resorted to a series of coercive measures known as War Communism.

- Over the course of 1918, industry was brought under state control. After 1918 nationalised industries operated under the overall supervision of the Supreme Council of National Economy, or *Vesenkha*, which had been established in December 1917. Headed by A.I. Rykov, the *Vesenkha* was attached to *Sovnarkom*. Individual industries were controlled by departments of the *Vesenkha*.

- The experiment with workers' control in the factories was ended. Workers' councils were scrapped. In their place came a return to traditional methods of management – 'one-man management', as it was called. In addition the Bolsheviks introduced internal passports in an attempt to halt the flight of industrial workers to the countryside. Trotsky wanted to go even further and impose military-style discipline on *Sovdepia*'s factory workers. Lenin, however, overruled him.

- From 1918 onwards food was requisitioned from the peasantry by the state. 'Food brigades' were sent out from the towns to extract grain from the peasantry and, where necessary, the Red Army and the *Cheka* were used. In practice 'requisitioning' often meant the straightforward theft of grain.

- Rationing was introduced. The way in which rationing worked reflected the Bolsheviks' priorities and values. The biggest rations went to Red Army soldiers and workers in heavy industry. Then came civil servants and workers in light industry, who received scarcely enough to live on. At the bottom of the scale came the middle classes.

Essential notes

The levels of brutality involved in grain requisitioning under War Communism can be seen in a telegram Lenin sent to Bolsheviks in Penza (about 640 km south-east of Moscow) who had problems with peasants hoarding grain.

'The uprising ... must be mercilessly suppressed ...

1. You need to hang (hang without fail, so that the people see) no fewer than 100 of the notorious kulaks [richer peasants], the rich and the bloodsuckers.
2. Publish their names.
3. Take all their grain from them.
4. [Pick out] the hostages – in accordance with yesterday's telegram.

This needs to be done in such a way that the people for hundreds of versts around will see, tremble, know and shout ...

PS Find tougher people.'

Examiners' notes

Examination questions focusing on the Russian Civil War are likely to ask you to weigh the importance of one cause of the Bolsheviks' victory in relation to others – for example, 'How significant was Trotsky's contribution to the Bolsheviks' victory in the Civil War?'

Remember, however, that questions may very well be set on the post-1917 period, which have a broader focus than the Civil War – though extensive reference to the Civil War will be expected in answers to them. Examples include 'To what extent were the weaknesses of their opponents responsible for the survival of the Bolshevik government in the years 1917–24?' and 'How far do you agree that the brutality of the Bolsheviks was the main reason why they remained in power in the years 1917–24?'

Why did the Bolsheviks win the Civil War?

There were four main reasons for the Bolsheviks' victory in the Civil War. Resources and geography were the most important of the four, which are discussed further below.

The Bolsheviks had more resources and a more favourable geographical position than their enemies.

Lenin's leadership.

Bolshevik victory in the Civil War

The Red Army's effectiveness as a fighting force.

Political failings and errors of the White Russian leadership.

Bolshevik victory in the Civil War. The green boxes indicate Bolshevik strengths; the orange indicates the weaknesses of the Bolsheviks' opponents

Resources and geography

In terms of resources and geography the Bolsheviks had three main advantages over their enemies.

The Bolsheviks and the Whites both relied on compulsory military service to raise their armies. However, the pool of manpower available to them differed considerably in size. The Bolsheviks controlled the most densely populated parts of Russia. In 1918–9 Bolshevik-held territory contained some 70 million people compared with approximately 20 million in the White-controlled areas.

Russia's main engineering factories were located within *Sovdepia* – notably the gigantic Putilov complex in Petrograd – giving the Bolsheviks the capacity to manufacture armaments. The Whites, by contrast, relied heavily on handouts from the Allies. The Bolsheviks also benefitted at the start of the Civil War from almost the whole of the arsenal of the old Tsarist army falling into their hands.

The Bolsheviks controlled the hub of the Russian railway network which radiated outwards from Moscow. This enabled the Bolsheviks to rush reinforcements to any battlefront on which they were seriously threatened. The Whites, in contrast, had to operate around the circumference of Bolshevik-held territory. Communications between the different White armies were limited, so it was virtually impossible for their commanders to coordinate their activities.

Political failings of the Whites

The White commanders proved to be incapable of mobilising popular support. This is not surprising: they were soldiers, not politicians. They knew little of popular opinion and underestimated the importance of propaganda.

There are a number of specific reasons why the White generals failed to attract an extensive following:

- They were divided. Some, for example, were monarchists while others wanted some sort of military dictatorship.

- Their message was negative rather than positive: other than anti-Bolshevism it was not entirely clear what they stood for.

- Their policy on the land issue. Influenced by the landowners among their supporters, Kolchak and Denikin made it known they intended to uphold property rights. Peasants were left in no doubt that a White victory would mean the restoration of land they had seized in 1917 to its former owners. Bolshevik propaganda was quick to play upon these peasant anxieties.

- Their brand of nationalism. The Whites believed in a Russia 'Great, United and Indivisible' – in other words, they wanted to re-establish Russia with its pre-1917 borders. They were unwilling to make concessions to separatists. This was a problem because some of the areas in which the White generals were based – the Ukraine and Transcaucasia – were ones in which separatist feeling was strong. Ukrainians and Georgians wanting self-government were never going to be enthusiastic supporters of White generals who were hostile to their aspirations.

Trotsky and the Red Army

Trotsky's contribution to victory was immense. He was not a great battlefield commander, but he built the Red Army out of nothing and moulded it into a disciplined and effective fighting force. In addition, he was an inspirational figure, moving from front to front in his famous armoured train, rallying Red troops with rousing speeches.

Remember that the Red Army was much bigger than the White forces. In most Civil War battles the Red Army enjoyed a huge numerical advantage.

Some of the Red Army's commanders were exceptionally talented.

Lenin's leadership

At first sight Lenin's role in the Civil War was a low-profile one. He remained in Moscow throughout, never visiting any of the battlefronts. He was nevertheless a key decision-maker.

- He forced through acceptance of Brest-Litovsk in the face of stiff opposition from other Bolsheviks.

- He was instrumental in the decision to construct a Red Army on traditional lines as opposed to relying on a people's militia.

- He presided over the introduction of War Communism.

- He was the driving force behind the use of methods of terror and gave the *Cheka* unwavering support.

The Bolsheviks did not win the Civil War because they themselves were popular. Their 'iron rule', as Lenin called it, won them few friends. However, the Bolsheviks appeared to many Russians to be defenders of the revolution against those who wished to turn the clock back, and when the Civil War crystallised into a Red-White conflict this proved to be a major advantage.

Essential notes

The point of maximum danger for the Bolsheviks in the Civil War was in 1919: the danger would have been greater still if Kolchak and Denikin had been able to synchronise their attacks.

Essential notes

The White generals had political advisers, but they were mostly nonentities. The most influential figures among the anti-Bolsheviks all exiled themselves from Russia during the Civil War era – Guchkov, Kerensky, Milyukov, Martov and Chernov.

Essential notes

In total the various White generals had around 250 000 men at their disposal. The Red Army numbered 400 000 in 1919 and over 5 million by 1921.

The Red Army's best general was Mikhail Tukhachevsky, who served as a junior officer in the Tsarist army in the 1914–7 war.

From War Communism to the NEP

The end of the Civil War brought no respite to the Bolshevik regime. In 1921 the Bolsheviks were confronted with a major internal crisis – one of their own making. Its immediate cause was widespread hostility to the policy of War Communism, but it owed much to more general disillusionment with Bolshevik rule. Lenin handled the crisis with characteristic skill, but its end result – the New Economic Policy (NEP) – was viewed with suspicion by many of his Bolshevik followers.

1921: Challenges to Bolshevism
Peasant revolt

During the Civil War, peasant hostility to grain requisitioning was to some extent kept in check by fears of a White victory. In 1920, however, as the fighting wound down and a poor harvest reduced villages to near-starvation, it boiled over. By 1921 much of the countryside was in revolt against Bolshevik rule. The government's response, spearheaded by the Red Army, was brutal: poisoned gas was used against rebels and thousands of women and children were taken hostage.

The effect of the uprisings was to bring Russia close to paralysis. Large parts of the country were effectively out of the authorities' control, the railways were seriously disrupted, there was a food crisis in the towns and the Red Army was stretched to the limit. In these circumstances Lenin had little alternative but to make concessions to the peasantry.

Urban protest

Urban protest was largely fuelled by food shortages, but there were also calls for the restoration of trade union rights, lost under War Communism, and allegations of widespread corruption within the Bolshevik Party. Anger in the towns expressed itself mainly in the form of strikes. In Moscow and Petrograd in 1921 there were clashes between troops and strikers in which people were killed.

The Kronstadt revolt

The Bolsheviks suffered a further blow in March 1921 when the 10 000 sailors of the Baltic fleet based at Kronstadt mutinied in support of the Petrograd strikers. The mutineers published a 15-point manifesto (sometimes called the *Petropavlovsk* Resolution, named after the battleship on which it was drafted) which condemned Bolshevik abuses of power. The manifesto called for the legalisation of all socialist and anarchist parties, new soviet elections, rights for trades unions and an end to special privileges for Bolshevik Party members.

From the Bolshevik point of view this was acutely embarrassing. In 1917 the Kronstadters had been among the Bolsheviks' strongest supporters: Trotsky had called them 'the pride and glory of the Russian Revolution'. Their mutiny in 1921 indicated just how extensive disillusionment with the Bolsheviks had become.

Discontent inside the Bolshevik Party

In 1920–1, two separate opposition groups emerged within the Bolshevik Party:

- the Democratic Centralists, who deplored the increasingly bureaucratic nature of Bolshevism

- the Workers' Opposition, who disliked the way in which the return to 'one-man management' under War Communism weakened the influence of trade unions.

The New Economic Policy

In March 1921 Lenin announced that grain requisitioning, or *prodraszverstka*, was to be abandoned. This was the first step in the introduction of the New Economic Policy (NEP). Other changes followed in piecemeal fashion over the next 18 months. The transition to the NEP was complete by the end of 1922.

The NEP created a mixed economy in Soviet Russia. A mixed economy is one in which there is both a public (or state-controlled) sector and a private sector which operates on the basis of the 'market forces' of supply and demand.

The NEP had four main features, as shown below.

Essential notes

The Democratic Centralists were mostly little-known intellectuals, but the Workers' Opposition was headed by two former members of *Sovnarkom*: Alexandra Kollontai, daughter of a Tsarist general and pioneer feminist, who was Commissar for Social Welfare in 1917–18, and Alexander Shlyapnikov, who was Commissar for Labour in 1917–8.

Grain requisitioning was replaced by a 'tax in kind'. This meant that peasants had to hand over to the state a fixed proportion of the grain they produced. Any surplus left over after this 'tax in kind' had been paid could be sold for profit on the open market. In 1924 the 'tax in kind' was replaced by money payments.

Private trading and the private ownership of small-scale businesses were legalised. Many of the privately-owned businesses which emerged under these arrangements were in the service sector – shops, market stalls, cafes, for example – but there was also a fair amount of private manufacturing. Privately-manufacturing companies typically produced consumer goods such as clothes and footwear.

NEP

Industries that remained under state control after 1921–22 were expected to trade at a profit and if they got into difficulties they were not bailed out by the government. One of the consequences of this new regime was an increase in unemployment as state-run industries shed surplus workers in order to increase efficiency.

The 'commanding heights' of the economy, as Lenin called them, remained under state control. The 'commanding heights' included not only heavy industries such as coal and steel but also the railway network and the banking system. Foreign trade continued to be a state monopoly.

Features of the NEP

NEP Russia, 1921–4

The key features of NEP Russia were economic recovery, political repression and a tightening of state control in areas such as religion and the arts.

Economic recovery

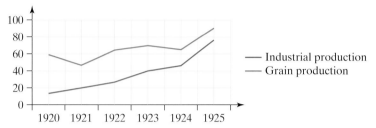

Economic recovery under the NEP

Note that the graph does not show *amounts* produced, but production expressed as a proportion of its 1913 level, with 1913 production being expressed in the form of a base of 100.

- The NEP was introduced too late to prevent a major famine. In mid-1921 a drought in the 'Black Earth' region led to crop failures. As a result of the requisitioning policy under War Communism, peasant households were left with no reserves of grain to fall back on. The consequence was a famine affecting 25 million people: the death toll may have reached as high as 5 million.

- The NEP nevertheless proved to be a success both politically and economically – from Lenin's point of view, at least. Politically it took the steam out of peasant discontent. Economically it brought about recovery. By the time of Lenin's death in 1924, the output of industry was rising sharply and grain production had risen well above the catastrophically low levels of 1920–1, although there had not been a return to pre-1914 levels of production in either industry or agriculture.

- Russia's economic recovery was erratic and uncertain rather than smooth and unbroken. Difficulties arose in 1923 because agriculture recovered more quickly than industry from War Communism. The price of food, relatively plentiful, fell: the price of consumer and manufactured goods, relatively scarce, rose. Trotsky called this the 'scissors crisis'.

- An unwelcome consequence of the NEP, so far as loyal Bolsheviks were concerned, was the emergence of a class of get-rich-quick private businessmen who were quick to flaunt their new wealth – so-called 'nepmen'. This they did in the bars, nightclubs and casinos that re-opened in Russia's major cities. It was a spectacle that angered many Bolsheviks. A comment popular among disillusioned Bolsheviks at the time was that the initials NEP really stood for 'New Exploitation of the Proletariat'.

Essential notes

'We felt as though the Revolution had been betrayed, and it was time to quit the Party. Capitalism is returning, we said, and money and the inequality we fought against are back.'

Alexander Barmine, a young Bolshevik in 1921, recalling discussions with his comrades on the introduction of the NEP

When Lenin introduced the NEP he did not pretend it was anything other than a surrender of principle for the sake of survival. It was, he said, a 'tactical retreat' and a 'peasant Brest-Litovsk'. The message was clear: the NEP was a temporary measure, to be abandoned in due course in favour of an authentically socialist policy. However, on the issues of how long the NEP would last and exactly what would replace it Lenin remained largely silent. These were issues that remained unresolved at the time of his death.

Political repression

One danger attached to the introduction of the NEP from the Bolshevik viewpoint was that the relaxation of state control in the economic sphere would give rise to expectations of a similar relaxation in the political sphere. Lenin's response was to make it clear that there would be no let-up in 'iron rule'. The introduction of the NEP was accompanied by a tightening of the Bolsheviks' political grip on Russia.

- The SRs and Mensheviks, just about tolerated in the Civil War era, were now suppressed.
- The *Cheka*, rebranded in 1922 as the GPU, enlarged its network of camps for political detainees.

Religion

Another way in which the Bolsheviks made it clear there was to be no softening of 'iron rule' was a renewed onslaught on the Orthodox Church.

The Orthodox Church had initially come under attack from the Bolsheviks in their first year in power. In 1917–18 the Church was stripped of its privileged status. It was separated from the state, its lands were confiscated, it was banned from owning property and it lost control of its schools. All monasteries were closed down and their assets seized. The head of the Church was put under house arrest. In the Civil War era, however, Bolshevik pressure on the Orthodox Church decreased.

The pretext for the Bolsheviks' new offensive against the Orthodox Church in 1921–2 was the claim that it had refused to sell its treasures to assist famine victims. Soviets were ordered to remove all precious items from churches in their localities. In many places priests and congregations resisted. This led to clashes between congregations and the Bolshevik authorities, in which some 8000 people were killed.

There followed two major 'show trials' in Moscow and Petrograd, in which prominent churchmen were accused of involvement in counter-revolution. These show trials were accompanied by a programme of harassment and ridicule of worshippers carried out by *Komsomol*, the Young Communist movement.

Essential notes

Bolshevik hostility to the Orthodox Church had two main roots.

- The Bolsheviks viewed all organised religion as an instrument used by ruling classes to deceive the masses into accepting their inferiority without complaint. In the Bolsheviks' view the elimination of religious belief would liberate the people from damaging superstition.
- The Bolsheviks believed that the Orthodox Church's close links with Tsarism made it a counter-revolutionary institution.

☞ Continued on the next two pages

Censorship and the arts

The Bolsheviks came to power at a time of exceptional creativity in the arts in Russia – especially the visual arts, where the likes of Kandinsky, Chagall, Malevich and Rodchenko were at work.

From the outset the Bolsheviks made extensive use of the visual arts for propaganda purposes. They were able to enlist the support of some of Russia's leading artists, notably Alexander Rodchenko.

In the early years of their rule the Bolsheviks allowed writers and artists a fair amount of freedom. Anatoly Lunarcharsky, the Commissar for Public Enlightenment, was a cultured and relatively tolerant figure who recognised that artists were not natural conformists and needed scope for self-expression.

State control of the arts became tighter in the early 1920s. During the Civil War era censorship in Russia was patchy and inefficient, but in 1922 it was put on to a new footing when the Directorate for Literature and Publishing, popularly known as *Glavlit*, was formed. After 1922 all items intended for publication needed a licence from *Glavlit* before they could appear. *Glavlit* also had responsibilities for suppressing 'underground' literature and here it worked closely with the *Cheka*.

Women and the family

The Bolshevik leadership prided itself on its advanced and progressive attitude to the issues of women's rights, divorce and sexual conduct. Soon after coming to power they swept away the restrictions on divorce and abortion which had existed in Tsarist Russia.

- In 1918 it became possible for a marriage to be dissolved at the request of either partner, without any need for grounds (such as desertion, cruelty or adultery) to be given.

- In 1920 abortion, strictly prohibited in Tsarist Russia, was legalised and made available free of charge in Soviet hospitals.

Soviet citizens, especially in the towns, took advantage of the new divorce and abortion laws in large numbers. In the mid-1920s Soviet Russia had the highest divorce rate in Europe. Abortion too became common: in 1926 nearly five per cent of all women of child-bearing age in Moscow had had an abortion. By the early 1930s Soviet doctors were performing 1.5 million abortions each year.

The extent to which these and other changes benefited Soviet women is open to question. Men and women may have been equal in the eyes of the law, but when state-run industries shed workers in the efficiency drive that followed introduction of the NEP:

- Women were made redundant in disproportionately large numbers.

- Women did not receive equal pay for equal work.

- Women deserted by the fathers of their children frequently struggled to get child support payments from them.

Essential notes

The number of women in the industrial workforce increased sharply in the Civil War era as a result of men being liable to compulsory military service. In 1921 45 per cent of all trade union members in Russia were women.

Was Lenin's Russia a totalitarian state?

Totalitarianism is a much-debated concept and it has no commonly agreed meaning. One widely used definition of totalitarianism, however, suggests that totalitarian countries have a number of key characteristics.

- There is an official state ideology.
- There is only one political party, usually headed by an all-powerful leader.
- The power of the state reaches into all aspects of the lives of citizens – there is no freedom of belief.
- There is a system of terroristic policing.
- The ruling party has total control of the means of mass communication – and of the armed forces.
- There is state control of all aspects of economic life.

Lenin's Russia was a totalitarian society in most, but not all, respects.

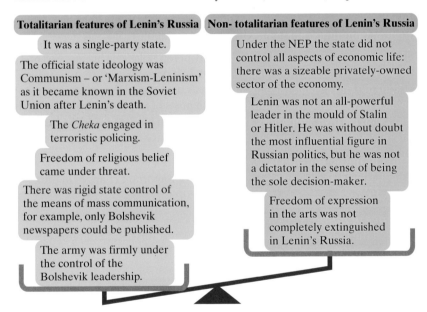

Totalitarian features of Lenin's Russia

It was a single-party state.

The official state ideology was Communism – or 'Marxism-Leninism' as it became known in the Soviet Union after Lenin's death.

The *Cheka* engaged in terroristic policing.

Freedom of religious belief came under threat.

There was rigid state control of the means of mass communication, for example, only Bolshevik newspapers could be published.

The army was firmly under the control of the Bolshevik leadership.

Non-totalitarian features of Lenin's Russia

Under the NEP the state did not control all aspects of economic life: there was a sizeable privately-owned sector of the economy.

Lenin was not an all-powerful leader in the mould of Stalin or Hitler. He was without doubt the most influential figure in Russian politics, but he was not a dictator in the sense of being the sole decision-maker.

Freedom of expression in the arts was not completely extinguished in Lenin's Russia.

Totalitarian and non-totalitarian features of Lenin's Russia

There is an argument which suggests that while early 1920s Russia was a largely totalitarian society it would not have remained so had Lenin lived beyond 1924. On this view, Lenin was an idealist who embraced totalitarian methods only because desperate circumstances forced him to, and who would have adopted a more liberal approach when Bolshevik power had been fully consolidated. There are difficulties with this interpretation. One of them, illustrated by the way the state tightened its control over cultural life after 1921, is that the Bolsheviks were as illiberal and repressive after the Civil War as they had been during it.

Essential notes

'Soviet historians accentuate the last period in Lenin's life. Here was Lenin apparently at his gentlest. Lenin of the New Economic Policy. Lenin the advocate of concessions to private enterprise. Lenin the opponent of bureaucrats. Nor was this an image of Lenin confined to the Soviet Union. Lenin as the embodiment of Soviet communism with a human face has been a widely reproduced picture in the West. The portrait bears little relation to reality. Bolshevism had a predisposition in favour of political, economic and social ultra-authoritarianism. Lenin advocated a milder variant of Bolshevism than Stalin. But it was still Bolshevism.'

Robert Service, 'Did Lenin lead to Stalin?'

Examiners' notes

The Specification covers up to 1924 – the year of Lenin's death. If you are answering a question on Bolshevik leadership, you can draw out the significance of his death and the years leading up to it. In May 1922 Lenin had a major stroke. In the two years before his death in 1924 he was a semi-invalid. In this stricken condition he turned his mind to the issue of the Bolshevik party leadership. In his 'Political Testament' (December 1922) he found fault with all of the main contenders – Trotsky, Stalin, Kamenev, Zinoviev, Bukharin – and appears to have hoped that after his death some sort of collective leadership would emerge.

Essential notes

The size of the Politburo in the Lenin era varied between 7 and 10 members. Lenin, Trotsky, Stalin, Kamenev and Bukharin were fixtures on the Politburo throughout 1919–24, but others came and went.

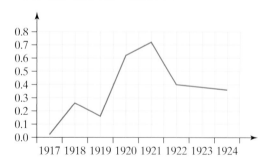

Bolshevik party membership, 1917–22 (millions)

Three key institutions: Party, secret police, Red Army

The nature of single-party rule in Lenin's Russia

The main pillar on which Bolshevik rule in the Lenin era rested was the Bolshevik Party itself. Two other important pillars were the Red Army and the *Cheka*, both of them subordinate to and controlled by the Bolshevik Party's leaders.

During the Lenin era, Bolshevik Party organisations grew in power at the expense of the institutions of the Soviet state. By 1924 all key decisions were being made by the Bolshevik Party's Political Bureau, or *Politburo*, established in 1919. The *Politburo* was a small 'inner cabinet' of about eight leading Bolsheviks. *Sovnarkom* and other state institutions such as government departments were sidelined: they were reduced to the role of implementing the *Politburo*'s decisions.

This process involved a loss of accountability. In the early days of Bolshevik rule, *Sovnarkom* was accountable to the Congress of Soviets (members of which were chosen by local soviets) and its Central Executive Committee. In the 1920s the *Politburo* was in theory answerable to the Bolshevik Party's Central Committee but in practice was accountable to no one.

The freedom from any real accountability of top Bolshevik leaders was one of the factors that allowed Stalin to build up a power base surreptitiously within the Party. Stalin used his position as the Party's General Secretary (which he held from 1922 onwards) to fill posts of responsibility at the local level with his own supporters. In the last years of his life Lenin became deeply worried about the way in which Stalin was accumulating power.

The changing Bolshevik Party, 1917–24

The Bolshevik Party underwent a number of important changes in the years 1917–24.

Change of name

In 1918 the Bolsheviks renamed themselves the 'Russian Communist Party (Bolsheviks)'. In relation to the Lenin era, the terms 'Bolshevik' and 'Communist' can be used interchangeably.

Growth in Party membership

Immediately before the February Revolution the Bolshevik Party had about 25 000 members. Over the next two years membership shot up to 350 000.

A purge of 'careerists' in late 1919 led to a temporary drop in numbers, but another phase of rapid growth followed which saw membership reaching 750 000 by 1921. Most of the new members were young, male and uneducated.

Centralisation of power

Before 1914 there was a culture of vigorous and open debate within the Bolshevik Party.

This culture continued to exist in and after 1917. In 1917, for example, Kamenev and Zinoviev questioned the wisdom of attempting to seize power in Petrograd, in 1918 Bukharin opposed acceptance of the Brest-Litovsk peace terms and in 1920–1 the Workers' Opposition called for a return to workers' control.

In 1921 the tradition of open debate was abruptly ended. Lenin announced a ban on the formation of factions within the Bolshevik Party.

The ban on factions arose out of the introduction of the NEP. Lenin knew that many Bolsheviks were strongly opposed to the NEP, seeing it as a return to capitalism and a surrender to Russia's anti-Bolshevik peasantry. These were not easy arguments for Lenin to counter. He therefore stifled debate by telling his critics that attacks on the decisions of the Party leadership were unacceptable.

The ban on factions was followed by a purge of the Party's membership. Around one-fifth of the Party's membership was expelled. Rank-and-file Bolsheviks were left in no doubt that what was expected of them was unquestioning obedience to the Party leadership. The Party's structure was now strongly hierarchical, with power concentrated at the top.

Secret police

Before 1917 Lenin repeatedly condemned the brutality of the Tsarist *Okhrana*. At no point was it suggested that a Bolshevik government might have need of a similar organisation. In the event, Bolshevik rule relied heavily on the secret police. The *Cheka* was a much larger organisation than the *Okhrana* and it was more brutal as well. It killed, tortured and imprisoned without trial far more people in 1917–24 than its Tsarist counterpart did in nearly one hundred years.

The Red Army

The Red Army was created to defend the Bolshevik revolution. This it did in the Lenin era in two ways.

- It fought conventional wars against the regime's enemies.
- It was involved in the suppression of internal opposition to the regime. It operated alongside the *Cheka* against the peasantry in the period 1918–21 and also put down the 1921 Kronstadt revolt.

The Bolsheviks were keen students of history. They were all too aware that the English and French revolutions of the 17th and 18th centuries had ended in military dictatorship. As a result they were determined to ensure that the Red Army remained firmly under Party control. This explains why they adopted the system of 'dual command' under which senior army officers had political commissars alongside them as minders.

Introduction

This section is intended to help you make the best use of your knowledge by applying it to particular situations. Although you need to have learned and understood the content of your course, you will not get many marks for simply repeating what you know. Questions always have a specific focus and you need to be able to identify this, select the best and most useful evidence and then apply it in a suitable way. This guidance should help you do this better.

The sections below will:

- show you how to interpret what a question is asking for
- help you decide which question will be your strongest
- show you how to structure and write your answer
- explain how the mark scheme works
- give some advice on how to plan your revision effectively.

The Unit 1 exam is based on Assessment Objective 1. It tests your ability to select relevant historical knowledge from what you have learned and to use it to support an argument that leads to a judgement based on the question you are tackling. The guidance given here will help you develop these skills.

In the exam, you will have 1 hour and 20 minutes to write two essays. You will have studied two of the seven topics on the paper. You will answer one question on each of your two topics. These notes cover D3, Russia in Revolution 1881–1924.

Working out the focus of the question

Understanding the words in the question

Always read the questions very carefully because each one has been put together to give you clues about how to answer it. Note any phrases used in the title and do not attempt a question unless you know what you are being asked to do.

Here is an explanation of the most common words and phrases that you will see. Make sure you know what they mean.

Question wording	Meaning
Responsible for	Causing to happen
Significant	Important
Outcome	Result
Course	The unfolding of events
Nature	What something is like
Turning point	Event after which things changed
Key features	Most important aspects
Transformation	Change of such significance that the whole nature of something is altered
Modernisation	Bringing up to date
Undergo	Experience

You will also be expected to know certain specialist historical terms that may come up in the question. Make sure you know what these mean.

Word	Definition
Tsarism	The system of government which the Tsar headed and the values it stood for – not just the Tsar as an individual
Revolution	Event or series of events, possibly violent, resulting in significant political, social or economic change
Repression	Use of harsh measures to keep control of people
Liberal	In general political terms, arguing for political change without violence, promoting the values of freedom and democracy
Conservative	In general political terms, defending traditional values and opposing change, unless it favours those already in power
Duma	Lower house of Russia's National Assembly, created in 1906
Coup	Seizing of power, usually by force
Provisional Government	The Duma committee that assumed power when Nicholas II abdicated, and was itself replaced by the Bolsheviks in November 1917
Bolsheviks	Lenin's faction within the Social Democrats, which successfully seized power in November 1917 and ruled Russia afterwards
Civil War	Struggle for power from 1919 to 1921 between the Bolsheviks and the various opposition forces
War Communism	Ruthless economic policy of the Bolsheviks during the Civil War, which involved grain requisitioning
Terror	Use of brutal methods against opponents

Listed below are some additional specialist terms that you are likely to need when constructing your answer. Make sure you are confident with them. Fill in the blank definition columns yourself and try to extend the list in the course of your studies.

Specialist term	Definition
July Days	The unsuccessful workers' and sailors' uprising in Petrograd in July 1917, crushed by the Provisional Government
Kornilov Coup	The unsuccessful attempt of the new commander-in-chief (Kornilov) to seize power from the Provisional Government in August 1917
Marxism	
Proletariat	
Bourgeoisie	
Slavophile	
Westerniser	
Constitution	
Soviet	
Kadet	
Menshevik	

Recognising the different types of question

Once you have seen a few past questions it will become obvious that there are certain types of question that are often set. You can break them down into three main types.

Questions focusing on causation

- Causation questions with a stated factor, in which you are asked to assess the importance of a stated factor alongside that of other factors.
- Causation questions asking 'why', without any stated factor, in which you are asked to explain the various reasons why something occurred and the links between them.

Questions focusing on change

- Assessing the extent of change
- Assessing the nature of change

Questions focusing on consequences

- Identifying and explaining the results, outcomes, consequences or impact of something on something else.
- Assessing the significance of something and explaining why it is important.

These are not watertight categories. There will be some overlap within each type of question. It is important that you can recognise the type of question you are doing so that you can structure your answer to tackle it directly. This applies particularly to 'consequence' questions. A common mistake is to start explaining the *causes* of a situation when you should actually be *assessing its consequences*. Below, each of these types of question is examined in more detail.

Causation questions with a stated factor

This is the most common type of question.

General points

To answer these questions, you need to weigh up the significance of the stated factor, alongside that of other factors that you must work out for yourself. It makes sense to start with the stated factor, then to broaden your response to deal with the others. You must make sure you address both in order to get a secure level 4 mark or above (see the explanation of the mark scheme, pages 85–7).

Sum up the significance of each factor you have discussed and comment on its relative importance. This will help to clarify your thoughts about the judgement that you will need to make in the conclusion.

Planned example

'How accurate is it to say that strong leadership was the main factor responsible for the consolidation of Bolshevik control of Russia, November 1917–24?'

In your introduction, make clear that you realise that consolidating Bolshevik control required more than just strong leadership and that a range of additional factors were responsible.

Do not just say there were other factors, identify them. Do not go into great detail yet. Factors such as taking pragmatic decisions (notably, making peace with Germany, giving peasants and workers what they wanted in late 1917 and dropping War Communism in favour of NEP), the use of terror, organising a centralised state and exploiting the various weaknesses of the 'Whites' would be important, although you may well find extra ones or break them down in a slightly different way.

For the stated factor, show that you understand that 'strong leadership' does not apply just to Lenin, but also to Trotsky and the whole culture of top-down leadership. Show also that you understand that the time frame covers the period immediately after the Bolshevik seizure of power until the death of Lenin – this was the crucial period for the survival of Communism.

Ideally, you should indicate how you intend to argue your case – whether you are putting most emphasis on the stated factor or one of the others. At this stage, you may want to keep your options open in the introduction. Make sure your argument is clear, though, by the time you reach the conclusion.

The main section should be a series of paragraphs devoted to each factor in turn, starting with the stated one of strong leadership.

For each factor, make a point, provide detailed supporting evidence and explain its relevance to the Bolshevik consolidation of power – then you will be answering the question directly. The table on the next page shows how you might go about it, but you will need to expand on the material in the *supporting evidence* column to ensure your point is well covered.

You may well decide that the stated factor deserves more than one paragraph, since you are never going to be given a stated factor that is not significant.

In your conclusion you need to reach a clear judgement about the relative importance of the factors you have discussed and explain your reasoning. If you have selected the stated factor as the main reason, reiterate *why* you see 'strong leadership' as essential to Bolshevik consolidation, and *which element of it* you see as most important. Try also to comment on how things changed over time. You could stress that leadership was most needed in the first months after the seizure of power, the time when the Bolshevik grip on power was at its most fragile – once the Civil War was won, survival was more likely.

Remember to highlight the links between the factors you have discussed. Point out that the leaders were putting other factors into operation – for example, without such strong leadership it would not have been possible to bring in the pragmatic policy changes or control the terror.

Remember:

- indicate how you intend to argue your case in the introduction
- reach a clear judgement in your conclusion.

In each paragraph think **PEER**:

- point
- evidence
- explained relevance to the question.

Point	Supporting evidence	Explained relevance to question – how did it help to consolidate control?
Stated factor Culture of strong leadership always an integral part of Bolshevism	They had seized power on behalf of workers at time of Bolsheviks' choosing; they never had been democrats	Meant leaders would not hesitate to act decisively as and when required
Stated factor Lenin: his capacity to take tough – if necessary, unpopular – decisions and his domination inside the Bolshevik Party	His decision to close Constituent Assembly in January 1918 as soon as it became clear Bolsheviks in minority – 175 Bolsheviks out of 717 seats He overruled opponents and agreed terms of Brest-Litovsk He set pace of anti-clerical persecution His ban on factions within Bolshevik Party in 1921	Constituent Assembly could have restricted what Bolsheviks did if allowed power – closure frightened elements of opposition and made it easier for Bolsheviks to impose their will Showed Lenin won most arguments inside CP and could defeat powerful men such as Trotsky and Bukharin Orthodox Church a powerful focus of alternative values Made organising internal opposition illegal
Stated factor Other leaders: Trotsky, Dzerzhinsky and Stalin	Trotsky's creation of disciplined and professional Red Army in Civil War, using political Commissars and enforcing brutal control over waverers; manipulation of ex-Tsarist officers Dzerzhinsky as *Cheka* chief Stalin's treatment of Georgia as Commissar for Nationalities	Army had disintegrated by 1918 and could not have won Civil War without being drastically reorganised; Trotsky's personal involvement inspirational Shows it was not just Lenin – strong leadership was normal at top of party
Other factor (1) Key pragmatic decisions Brest-Litovsk Land and workers' control decrees 1917 Abandoning War Communism in favour of NEP 1921	Lenin's insistence on immediate peace with Germany whatever the cost, overruling Trotsky Land decree gave peasants right to seize land though technically it belonged to 'the state'; workers' control decree gave factory committees supervisory powers Requisitioning of grain causing serious urban food shortages and provoking unrest from peasants in Tambov province and workers and sailors in Kronstadt	Enabled Bolsheviks to focus on eradicating internal enemies and dealing with key domestic issues Both went beyond what Bolsheviks had intended but it made sense to concede these early and claw back control later once they were secure in power; made Bolshevism seem more attractive than any White alternative to most of population War Communism had fed Red Army in Civil War but risked provoking a counter-revolution from peasants and workers if it continued; NEP restored incentives to peasantry and led to boost in grain production for a while
Other factor (2) Use of terror	Terror an integral part of Bolshevik approach – used against all opponents and ruthlessly enforced by *Cheka* (then GPU) and Red Army Class warfare by general public encouraged – physical attacks on 'bourgeoisie'	Creation of climate of fear deterred opposition and removed potential alternative leaders – royal family executed 1918; even used against Kronstadt rebels before concessions granted under NEP
Other factor (3) Creating a centralised state	Creation of USSR; key Bolshevik Party organs (Politburo) and state (*Sovnarkom*) with decisions in hands of small number in elite of Bolshevik Party	Power vacuum after Provisional Government fell and Constituent Assembly dissolved Quick creation of new organs essential, as was a federal state that could accommodate national minorities
Other factor (4) Exploitation of weaknesses of 'Whites' (non-Bolsheviks)	Military weaknesses – failure of Kolchak, Deniken and Yudenich to work together in Civil War, half-hearted nature of foreign aid Lack of popular appeal to land-hungry peasants gaining from land decree Image of being under foreign leadership a propaganda opportunity to Reds	Victory in Civil War essential, otherwise Bolsheviks simply would not have survived in power

Causation questions asking 'why?', without any stated factor

General points

It is important to group your reasons logically and to give each one appropriate weighting according to its significance. Remember to keep linking your reason back to the focus of the question. Avoid producing an answer that reads like a list of potential reasons with little comment on the significance of each one. Make sure your judgement is explicitly stated in the conclusion.

These questions may look very straightforward but can be deceptive. They usually include a twist of some kind, for example, 'Why, despite x, did a certain outcome result?' or 'Why did a certain development occur at a certain time?'

Planned example

'Why did opposition to Tsarism turn into a serious revolution so quickly during 1905?'

One reason why the revolution was so serious was the speed with which it developed but there are plenty of other reasons that you should explain. You will need to put the 1905 events into context because the grievances that motivated the revolutionaries had been building for some time.

This particular question is asking you to explain two inter-related things.

- Why did discontent escalate so *quickly*?
- What made it such a *serious revolution* as far as the government was concerned?

In your introduction, select events from 1905 to show that you understand that the Revolution was both 'serious' and 'quick'. For example, the 'Bloody Sunday' massacre of January sparked off disturbances that developed rapid momentum, peaking in October with a general strike in St Petersburg and forcing Tsar Nicholas to make serious concessions. Then he was able to crush the industrial workers by force in December.

However, the focus of the question is 'Why?' so you must base your answer on reasons. Identify these; for example, the 'Bloody Sunday' massacre itself, the high level of industrial unrest in early 1905, the peasantry's economic fears, liberal political frustration, national minority anger at years of Russification and the humiliating military defeats being inflicted by Japan were all significant contributory factors to the situation.

Also, identify the key reasons why it seemed such a serious revolution – that the different groups were for the first time apparently working together while the army was absent at war. Normal economic grievances seemed to be getting political, especially when the St Petersburg Soviet was set up.

In the main section each paragraph must explain a relevant reason. You could group your explanations along the lines suggested here.

There were three key reasons why unrest escalated so fast in 1905.

1. Because Bloody Sunday was so shocking – Nicholas chose not to return to the Winter Palace to receive the petition, and his guards killed over 200 peaceful protestors who were led by a priest. This shattered his image as the 'Little Father' who cared for the wellbeing of ordinary Russians.

2. Because of its timing – coming just after the fall of Port Arthur, the crucial defeat in a war which the Russians had expected to win. This damaged Nicholas' reputation as ruler and increased liberal frustration at being unable to contribute to more effective government. It also coincided with serious industrial unrest in St Petersburg where 100 000 workers were on strike.

3. Because the ingredients for serious unrest were already there. High levels of economic discontent among peasants anxious about high taxation and frustrated by the difficulty of buying more land meant outbreaks of peasant disorder were frequent anyway.

   - Poor working and living conditions in the growing industrial centres were inevitably causing discontent which the government was trying to head off by encouraging non-Marxist trade unions.

   - National minority and Jewish grievances had been simmering since Alexander III began his policy of Russification, so this was an ideal chance for them to make a bid for freedom.

   - Liberals had been frustrated at their exclusion from government since Alexander III had restricted *zemstva* powers and Nicholas had made clear his opposition to any elected parliament. They had been using their banquet campaign to get round censorship restrictions in 1904.

You could identify three main reasons why it became a 'serious revolution'.

1. The sheer scale of the unrest was unprecedented – strikes among industrial workers and students spread to most cities, even beyond European Russia. By October there was a general strike in St Petersburg. Peasant attacks on landlords reached high levels in the Black Earth and Volga regions. The Socialist Revolutionaries assassinated Grand Duke Sergei. Georgia descended into anarchy.

2. The signs of increased revolutionary organisation and the impression that the various strands of opposition were acting together for the first time – a new Peasant Union was formed and affiliated itself to the liberal-led Union of Unions; the St Petersburg workers created the Soviet, electing Trotsky as chairman. This also gave the economic grievances a definite political edge, which was much more serious a threat.

3. The difficulty for the authorities in keeping law and order while the bulk of the military were at war with Japan. Normally the army helped maintain internal law and order, but now there were insufficient troops to do so – and their loyalty was being stretched by the defeats, as highlighted by the *Potemkin* mutiny.

You might also include Nicholas' slow reaction, which allowed events to build up impetus. Bulygin's August proposals were not enough for the liberals and it took Witte to extort the October Manifesto from Nicholas.

In your conclusion you need to sum up the main reasons why there was so much unrest and why it was so serious. The key points are that it was a combination of forces apparently working together through the Union of Unions, the unprecedented scale of the unrest and the absence of large sections of the military, which in peace time was essential in helping preserve law and order.

Change questions: assessing the extent of change

General points

You need to work out how much certain things changed over a specified time period and identify things that hardly changed at all. You must show awareness of the more subtle differences, depending on what is being discussed.

Planned example

'To what extent was Russia changed by the reforms brought in between 1906 and 1914?'

In your introduction, identify the main reforms that you will later be assessing in detail. In terms of political reform, these cover the granting of greater freedom of expression in the October Manifesto promises, then the Fundamental Laws of 1906, which clawed power back for the Tsar, and how the new political system operated in practice. In economic terms, the main changes concerned the impact of Stolypin's land reform on the peasantry. Some other social reforms covered education and health insurance for workers. Indicate how you will be arguing in terms of the extent of change.

In your main section, you might deal with the changes thematically, discussing political, economic and social areas in turn. This is the approach outlined below.

> Avoid bland comments such as 'politics changed a lot'. Break things down so you can make more telling comments and contrast the rates of change in different areas or at different times in the given period.

Reform	Change	Continuity
Political freedom	Political parties legalised Duma created as National Consultative Assembly with elections being held for first time Press censorship relaxed	Fundamental Laws 1906, reiterating Tsar's ultimate authority and limited role of the Duma Article 87, providing for rule by decree when Duma not sitting Changes to electoral law after second Duma 1907 Continued harsh treatment of political agitators
Economic reform – Stolypin's land reform	Reduced power of *mir* by making it possible to opt out and consolidate holdings, and so on Peasant Land Bank facilitated loans for land purchase and migration eastwards to colonise Steppes and western Siberia Ending redemption payments slightly early Promotion of new techniques, machinery, and so on, and the encouragement of cooperatives	Slow bureaucratic process Old mentalities too well entrenched to change quickly Issue of whether Stolypin's assassination in 1911 was a sign that Nicholas wanted to stop reforms
Social reform	1908 Education reform theoretically set up basic primary education for all 8–11-year-olds big expansion in secondary and higher education Central government spending more than doubled by 1914 1912 accident and health insurance for some workers, mainly financed by employers *Zemstva* more actively trying to use their powers to improve health and education in regions	Russia still lagged far behind Western powers in education spending and provision by 1914 Failure of Duma efforts to free Church from state influence and to reduce peasant drunkenness

It can be useful to divide your response into short- and long-term impact, since effects vary as time passes. For example, the impact of some factors lessened in intensity over time, as in the case of enthusiasm for the First World War; it was high in 1914 but had dwindled by 1916. In contrast, the impact of social and economic grievances with Tsarism grew over time and was then triggered into revolution in 1905 by Bloody Sunday.

The planned example below can be treated in a similar way to a causation question since it requires you to weigh up the relative impact of a range of consequences on the Provisional Government's future chances.

In your conclusion, you can reinforce your judgement by restating areas where change was greatest and areas where continuity was more typical.

Change questions: assessing the nature of change
General points
For these questions, you need to discuss the nature of change (whether there was progress or modernisation, whether something grew stronger or weaker and so on).

Planned example
The mind map on page 79 gives a good illustration of how you might plan for a question of this type.

Consequences questions: assessing the impact
General points
These questions require you to explain the impact of something on something else. The wording may vary between consequences, effects, results, outcome, and so on, but the theme is what happened because of another event. You should focus on the stated factor's impact, but do not confine your answer to this – you should also discuss other relevant factors that caused an impact.

Planned example
'How far do you agree that the decision to continue the war made the survival of the Provisional Government impossible?'

In your introduction, identify the wide range of problems *directly caused by this decision*: difficulty in organising elections, continued problems feeding cities, danger of unsettling the army if they authorised land redistribution, failure of the June Brusilov Offensive and rivalry with Petrograd Soviet being important ones. Then point out the problems that came *indirectly from the decision*, due to Lenin's return and his success in getting the Bolsheviks to use the Soviet as an alternative to the Provisional Government. Make it clear that there were also other factors *not directly linked to the decision* that placed its survival in jeopardy: their liberal approach to opposition, their claim to be provisional rather than permanent, their lack of legitimacy as a remnant of the old Duma.

In your main section, take each problem that the decision caused, or made worse, and link it to the war and the impact it had on the future survival of the Provisional Government. Deal also with other problems they faced: those indirectly resulting from the decision to fight on (yellow highlighting), or not resulting from the decision (purple highlighting) (see table opposite). These are not watertight distinctions so be prepared to make cross-references between them.

In your conclusion, ensure you have reached a judgement about the extent to which the decision to continue fighting the war contributed to the Provisional Government's downfall.

Problem	How war made the problem worse	Impact on Provisional Government's chances of survival
Delayed elections	Decided to delay elections since so many soldiers away and organisation possibly too disruptive	Meant they could not claim to be legitimate government representing the entire people; Soviet could claim to represent more people numerically
Delayed land reform	Fearing that transfer of land from aristocracy to peasantry would unsettle peasant soldiers and lead to desertions in order to participate; held an inquiry into it but did nothing	Delays alienated peasantry who began to seize land once army discipline broke down after June; countryside out of their control by November; Lenin and SRs both promising land to peasantry
Lack of food supplies to cities	Army took priority and transport system was dislocated so cities continued to be short of supplies	Shortages had been short-term cause of Petrograd disturbances, which brought down Tsar in March; same problem on horizon for next winter; Lenin promised bread
Launching a new offensive (and losing)	Decision to take military initiative and try to make war a revolutionary crusade had not inspired soldiers to victory; desertions increased	Defeats meant Provisional Government seen as no more effective at waging war than Tsar had been; discipline in army breaking down, soldiers deserting to seize land
July Days Uprising	Failure of June Offensive was catalyst that sparked off serious unrest in Petrograd	Should actually have helped Provisional Government since they suppressed it and then portrayed demonstrators as traitors
Handling of Kornilov Coup	He had been (unwisely) promoted to commander-in-chief following Brusilov's failed offensive and so had military units at his disposal	Over-reaction by Provisional Government – lost initiative gained in July, allowed Bolsheviks to rebuild support by releasing Bolshevik prisoners and calling for mass resistance to Kornilov
Rivalry with Soviet once Lenin returned (April)	War that made Germans facilitate Lenin's return; Soviet sought to claim army loyalty (rather than that of workers)\n\nLenin backed Soviet and stopped dual authority	Doubt over who army would obey – their stance crucial in Tsar's loss of control in March; Soviet became a rival to Provisional Government
Lenin's (and Trotsky's) ability to organise Bolsheviks	Lenin promised what Provisional Government did not – peace, bread, land; Bolsheviks gradually took over Soviet; Lenin persuaded Bolsheviks to stage coup, organised by Trotsky	Made it increasingly hard for Provisional Government to command loyalty of urban workers and peasants
Its claim to be provisional	War delayed vital decisions (above) that needed taking quickly before initial popularity evaporated	The longer it lasted the less credibility it would have, especially as its support base was so narrow
Their liberal approach – allowed free speech and alternative views to flourish	Failures due to war provided ammunition for critics; rivals could organise opposition	Made it easy for challengers to attack them; tried to suppress Bolshevik press in November, but too late

Consequence questions: assessing the significance of change

General points

These have some similarities with other types of question, in that you are being asked to weigh up the way a specified factor impacted on something else. It is important to focus on the stated factor since you will not be asked to assess the significance of something unimportant. However, you might broaden your answer to discuss other factors that had an impact.

Planned example

'How significant were Nicholas II's own misjudgements in bringing about the fall of Tsarism in March 1917?'

In your introduction, show you understand why Nicholas' misjudgements contributed to the downfall of Tsarism, by identifying his main errors. Many factors can be linked to his decision to take over as commander-in-chief, based at the Front, his reluctance to trust the middle-class organisations that wanted to help run the war and to his conduct in early 1917. Do not ignore longer-term errors that might also have been significant, relating to the missed opportunities after 1905.

Wider factors might include aspects of the way Russia was changing, economically and socially, that were beyond Nicholas' control.

Misjudgements of Nicholas	Contribution to fall of Tsarism
In wartime	
Failure to trust middle class – initial suspension of Duma	Missed chance to harness their expertise and improve quality of government; eventually alienated people who wanted to help – Progressive Bloc became focus of criticism
Poor appointments to key government posts – succession of mediocre PMs	Meant Nicholas received poor advice and alienated more able ministers who were overlooked
Decision to assume personal military command 1915	Meant all defeats personally linked to him and was absent from Petrograd and reliant on Alexandra for updates on Home Front
Placing too much trust in Rasputin in particular	Image of government discredited – alienation of elite who eventually murdered him
Allowing Alexandra too much power in his absence	More damage to image of royal family as allegations of treason gathered pace
Failing to organise the transport system effectively, meaning there were serious food shortages in Petrograd by February 1917	Meant thousands of demonstrators on streets
In the longer term	
Failing to reform more urgently since 1906, to modernise agriculture and industry, to allow middle class more of a role in national government, to placate national minorities, and so on	Such long-term problems resurfaced as hardships of war dragged on and provided easy focal points for grievances in March 1917

Also continuation of autocracy inevitably meant Nicholas' failings had huge impact on Russia |

Other responsible factors	Their contribution
Petrograd garrison could not quell trouble in March 1917	Meant law and order could not be restored, prompting the Tsar to make major concessions
Appearance of Petrograd Soviet at same time as above	Increased difficulty Nicholas would have of reasserting control over workers and soldiers

In your conclusion you need to stress what the most serious misjudgement seems to have been, and why. Plenty of the problems he encountered can be linked together. The question asks about the fall of 'Tsarism', not just of Nicholas, so be prepared to show you know that no other Romanov stepped in when Nicholas himself abdicated.

Choosing the best question to tackle

Once you understand the differences between these three question types, it should be easier for you to choose the best question to tackle. If you can recognise the question types, you should be able to construct a quick outline plan based on the examples given in the preceding pages.

For example, for the question: *'How far did the Russian political system change between 1906 and 1914?'*, you should be able to work out that this is a nature of change question and you could plan it with a brief diagram, like this.

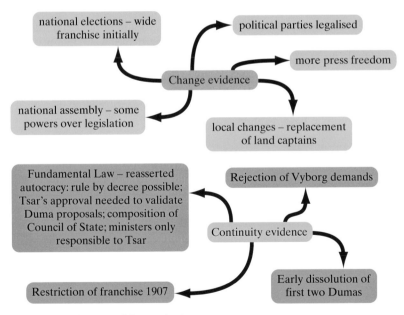

Evidence for change and for continuity

Structuring and writing an effective answer

In brief
Essays need to be structured into three sections: the introduction, the main body of the argument and the conclusion. Structuring your answer clearly is really important for two reasons: first, it helps the examiner follow your answer so they can give it the mark it deserves and second, it helps you keep focused on the question.

1. The introduction is important but should not be too long – five or six lines should be enough. You need to identify the range of factors you intend to discuss in the main section and to give an idea of how you intend to argue your case – the line of argument you intend to develop in the main section. If there are words in the title that need to be explained, then do this here. You also need to show you understand why any particular dates have been selected.

2. The main section should be a series of four to six developed paragraphs that will lead to a substantial conclusion. Start each paragraph with a point that you are making as part of your argument. You need to provide accurate and reasonably precise evidence to support the point and then explain clearly how it adds to your argument. This last requirement is often what students forget to do, so practise making your point explicitly relevant and keep referring back to the wording of the question to remind yourself what the argument is about. Remember to address both sides of the argument, such as continuity and change or the stated factor and the other factors.

3. The conclusion should sum up the points in your argument and make clear why you are arguing your case in this particular way. Do not suddenly throw in new ideas at this stage – the conclusion should follow on from what you have already written. It is a good idea to stress what you see as the crucial point in your case and why this is so. It is vital to have a conclusion so the examiner can see the overall judgement you have reached.

In detail
In the section that follows you will see relatively weak essay examples, followed by revised, stronger examples to illustrate how to structure and write an effective answer.

Introduction
Think about this question and read the responses that follow.

'How far do you agree that the decision to continue the war made the survival of the Provisional Government impossible?'

This is a reasonable start because it shows an understanding of the time period involved and that there was more to it than just the stated factor, so the general line of argument has been indicated. However, it does not say what these other reasons were and it does not give any indication of why the decision to continue fighting was so disastrous.

Weak example
The Provisional Government took over from Nicholas II when he abdicated in March, but it decided to carry on fighting the war, which was an important factor in bringing about its downfall. However there were also other factors that contributed to the Bolshevik coup in November, so it was not just the war decision that made the Provisional Government's survival impossible.

Strong example
The Provisional Government's decision to continue fighting the war certainly made its survival more unlikely because it meant they delayed introducing changes that people wanted, such as holding elections and redistributing land. However, it also fell for several other reasons, most of which were connected with Lenin's return and the way he undermined their position and ensured the Bolsheviks challenged their authority. No government would have found it easy to run Russia, given the problems faced in March 1917.

This is much better because it gives a clear idea of why the decision to fight on caused the Provisional Government problems. It also gives an idea of the nature of the additional problems that brought it down. Importantly, it avoids getting drawn into the kind of detail that can come later.

Main section
Deal with your most important point in the first paragraph. This will be the stated factor in a multi-factor question or the most significant factor in other types. The basic formula is to support your point with examples from your own knowledge and then make clear how this adds weight to your argument.

Weak example
One problem the war caused the Provisional Government was that it made them delay elections, fearing that it would be unfair not to let soldiers who were serving at the front have a vote. By the time the elections were held in November, the Bolsheviks had just seized power. Earlier elections would have made the Provisional Government more popular and helped avoid this.

While this is a reasonable paragraph, it does not offer much explanation or background. It does not say why it mattered so much that elections were delayed or why holding them sooner might have prolonged the Provisional Government's life. The next response is better because the importance of the point is explained and the final sentence makes it explicitly relevant to the survival of the government.

Strong example
A major problem caused by the decision to fight on in the war was that it made holding elections difficult since so many soldiers at the front line would be unable to vote. However, because the Provisional Government was just the remnants of the old Duma, elected on a narrow franchise, it could not claim to represent the people of Russia as a whole and so it lacked legitimacy. Until elections were held, critics could accuse it of only representing the well to-do classes and the longer they delayed the greater the resentment this caused. If Russia had no longer been at war, elections could have been held much sooner and this problem averted.

This response is better because the importance of the point is explained and the final sentence makes it explicitly relevant to the survival of the government. You should follow this approach to each paragraph, addressing a new point each time and, where possible, linking back to previous points to show you understand the connections.

In the best essays, one paragraph follows on naturally from the one before. You can do this by starting the new point with a comment that refers to what is said at the end of the previous paragraph. For example, after the paragraph above, you might launch the next one like this.

This shows that the war also delayed another change that the Provisional Government were expected to make, for broadly similar reasons. It also states what they did instead of redistributing land. You could then continue as shown.

In a similar way, the war encouraged the Provisional Government to delay redistributing land – again because of the damaging effect it might have on army morale if conscripted peasants thought they were missing out on getting land by staying at their posts in the army. Partly because they feared mass desertions, the Provisional Government held an enquiry into land reform but did nothing more.

Meanwhile the Socialist Revolutionaries were loudly demanding land reform, and Lenin had adopted the same tactics and was promising 'land', along with 'peace and bread' on behalf of the Bolsheviks. These promises were much more attractive to the peasants than the empty gestures of the Provisional Government and they eventually began to take the law into their own hands and seize land for themselves. Again this was a problem that could have been dealt with sooner if the war had ended but, because it was not, the Provisional Government lost control of the countryside and this seriously undermined their chances of survival.

This paragraph explains why the failure to redistribute land undermined their chances, using selected knowledge about the SRs and Bolsheviks to support the point. The final comment brings it back again to the wording of the question.

It is important to finish each point by linking back to the wording of the title in some way, almost like writing a mini-conclusion at the end of each paragraph. This should guarantee that you are addressing the question directly, which is what you need to be doing to get a mark within level 4 or 5.

Conclusion

The conclusion should round off all the points you have already made in your argument and make clear why you have argued your case in this particular way. Do not introduce a brand new point at this stage! Reaching a clear judgement is essential for good marks. Emphasise which point has been the most crucial in helping you reach that decision and why you consider it to be so important. If your argument used longer-term and shorter-term factors, go back to these to show that there were different factors operating at different points in time. Refer to any dates in the question here and make sure you are dealing with the whole time period.

If you find you have only 5 minutes left, and still have not started a conclusion, move straight on to it. You will get more marks this way because the examiner needs to see that you have reached an overall judgement. A reasonable conclusion for the question above might look like this.

This presents a judgement and gives a reason for the interpretation. However, it is unbalanced because it has not included the wider reasons.

Weak example
Continuing the war did make the Provisional Government's survival impossible because it forced them to delay elections and sort out the land redistribution issue, two mistakes that made them unpopular and so reduced their grip on power. As time passed it seemed that the war was stopping the new government solving Russia's main problems and so they were overthrown in November.

Strong example

The Provisional Government's decision to continue the war did undoubtedly make their chances of survival more difficult because it delayed them in proving their legitimacy and prevented them sorting out the land and food problems. These were serious mistakes, which led to a fall in their popularity after the euphoria of the first few weeks in the spring of 1917. However, their survival only became impossible because of the way that Lenin imposed his will on the Bolsheviks and got them to stop cooperating with the Provisional Government and support his plans for a coup.

This one shows the interaction between factors, as well as distinguishing between 'impossible' and 'difficult', which shows careful consideration of the judgement.

Key tips

Introducing new paragraphs

- Each paragraph needs to be based on a point in your argument. It will be more convincing if one point leads on to the next, so it is worth practising ways of starting new points that do this. If one point has elements in common with the one before, then show this by using 'In a similar way…'.

- Where you are moving to a different kind of point, start with 'In contrast…'.

- Sometimes the next point will reinforce the previous one, so try using 'Moreover…' or simply 'In addition…'.

- Try starting with 'Nevertheless…' when dealing with a contrasting situation.

- In the course of your paragraph you will need to emphasise the importance of the key points compared to the less important ones, so have a vocabulary at your disposal to help you create a sense of hierarchy. Words such as 'significant', 'major', 'decisive' and 'effective' can do this.

- Words such as 'strong', 'successful' and 'competent' convey much more accurate meaning than 'good'. Likewise, 'weak', 'unsuccessful' and 'incompetent' are much more expressive than 'bad'.

- If you are writing about the extent of change, starting a point with 'By…' followed by the date can be an effective way of summarising what had been achieved over a certain period of time. Looking back over developments from the end date can be a concise way of showing that you know the key events without writing a narrative.

- Remember that you will be making a judgement, so build up an appropriate vocabulary to help you express this.

Using specialist vocabulary and handling concepts sensibly

Your answers will be more convincing if you can use specialist terms appropriately. However, do not fall into the trap of using them excessively and unnecessarily – just be confident enough to use them when relevant.

Some of the mainstream terms that come up in essay titles were discussed earlier. There were also suggestions to get you started on building up your own specialist vocabulary to use in your answers (see page 69).

Using the appropriate level of detail

Dates

Dates are important, as history does not make sense without them, so know the years when significant things happened. In years when important things never seemed to stop happening (1905 and 1917), know the months as well. At the very least you need to know the order in which events happened. Using time charts as a revision tool (see page 88) can be a really effective way of learning dates. Occasionally students go too far and think they need the actual day of the month – this is hardly ever useful.

It is important to be able to stand back from events and see them in perspective – try to get used to seeing how details fit in to the bigger picture. Too much detail obscures the broader picture, but too little leads to a hazy, unclear picture. Knowing the key dates certainly helps with this.

Statistical evidence

This can be useful, especially if you are trying to show the extent of change. However, make sure that your figures have relevance – it is not much use just saying that there were 80 000 primary schools in Russia in 1914. However, if you then say there were only 45 000 in 1906 you can make a telling contrast and point out that the number had almost doubled in less than ten years. Round figures to a sensible degree of accuracy and remember to make clear why you have included them – what point are they intended to show?

Quotes

Using quotes can be a really convincing way of making a point, but always attribute them to the right person and if possible comment on the context in which the comment was made. If you cannot remember the exact words, you can still say what their comment reveals. For example, if you cannot remember what Nicholas II allegedly said about the Duma, in 1906 ('Damn the Duma – it is all Witte's work!'), it is still useful to say that after granting the Duma Nicholas made derogatory remarks about it and blamed it all on Witte. However, there needs to be some reason for pointing this out – in this case you could be showing that once Nicholas felt he had survived 1905, he wanted to go back on his promises.

Quotes from historians can also add weight to your argument, but make sure they come from experts in the appropriate particular field (such as Robert Service or Orlando Figes), not from textbooks or revision guides.

Geography

Some basic geographical knowledge is also useful in a topic such as this, since the Russian Empire was huge and included such diverse peoples and resources. Ensure you can refer to other key cities such as St Petersburg (Petrograd), Moscow, Baku, Kiev or Vladivostok. Answers on the economy will require you to know a bit about the Donets Basin, the Urals, Siberia,

Poland, the Black Earth regions and the Lena goldfields. The Civil War took place over a variety of battlefronts. You should also know where the most vociferous national minorities were located.

Writing legibly

Examiners can only award marks for what they can read. If your writing is so poor that the examiner cannot read it, this is will pull down your mark within a level because it will be seen as weak communication. (Check the mark scheme on pages 86–7.)

Saving time in an emergency

If you find that you really are running out of time in the exam and will not be able to finish the answer in the way you had hoped to, here are two strategies to minimise the damage.

Things to do

✓ Finish your main section with a plan that shows how each paragraph would have been structured: the point, a piece of supporting factual evidence and some words making this relevant to the wording of the question. This last piece of advice is essential because the examiner needs to see how you would be arguing the case – you must show how you would *use* a fact to make a point. A mind map may be useful provided you make clear how your argument would develop.

✓ Write a conclusion of reasonable length and ensure it includes a supported judgement.

Things not to do

✗ Write long slabs of description, not tailored to the wording of the question.

✗ Use abbreviations instead of people's names, institutions, and so on.

✗ Memorise lots of different historians' views on issues. The main thing is to know and understand the different ways that an event can be interpreted – you do not need to know which historian said what.

Understanding the mark scheme

The examiner puts each essay into one of five levels according to the criteria in the table on the next page. Your answer is then moved within the level, depending on how well it meets the descriptor. Obviously, you want to your answer to go into the highest possible level, so it is worth becoming familiar with the table so that you know what the examiners are looking for.

Level	Mark range	Mark scheme descriptor	What this means
1	1–6	Candidates will produce mostly simple statements. These will be supported by limited factual material, which has some accuracy and relevance, although not directed at the focus of the question. The material will be mostly generalised. There will be few, if any, links between the simple statements. **Low Level 1: 1–2 marks** The qualities of Level 1 are displayed; material is less convincing in its range and depth. **Mid-Level 1: 3–4 marks** As per descriptor. **High Level 1: 5–6 marks** The qualities of Level 1 are securely displayed; material is convincing in range and depth consistent with Level 1. The writing may have limited coherence and will be generally comprehensible, but passages will lack both clarity and organisation. The skills needed to produce effective writing will not normally be present. Frequent syntactical and/or spelling errors are likely to be present.	Answer will be made up of brief comments on the topic rather than on the question that has been set. Is likely to be generalised and inaccurate. Will be poorly written in a simple style.
2	7–12	Candidates will produce a series of simple statements supported by some accurate and relevant factual material. The analytical focus will be mostly implicit and there are likely to be only limited links between the simple statements. Material is unlikely to be developed very far. **Low Level 2: 7–8 marks** The qualities of Level 2 are displayed; material is less convincing in its range and depth. **Mid-Level 2: 9–10 marks** As per descriptor. **High Level 2: 11–12 marks** The qualities of Level 2 are securely displayed; material is convincing in range and depth consistent with Level 2. The writing will have some coherence and will be generally comprehensible, but passages will lack both clarity and organisation. Some of the skills needed to produce effective writing will be present. Frequent syntactical and/or spelling errors are likely to be present.	Answer shows some understanding of the question topic but knowledge has not been directed at the wording of the question. Material will be more accurate than at Level 1. Points raised are not explained. Again, poorly written but better organised in terms of paragraphs than at Level 1.
3	13–18	Candidates' answers will attempt analysis and will show some understanding of the focus of the question. They will, however, include material which is either descriptive, and thus only implicitly relevant to the question's focus, or which strays from that focus. Factual material will be accurate but it may lack depth and/or reference to the given factor. **Low Level 3: 13–14 marks** The qualities of Level 3 are displayed; material is less convincing in its range and depth. **Mid-Level 3: 15–16 marks** As per descriptor. **High Level 3: 17–18 marks** The qualities of Level 3 are securely displayed; material is convincing in range and depth consistent with Level 3. The writing will be coherent in places but there are likely to be passages which lack clarity and/or proper organisation. Only some of the skills needed to produce convincing extended writing are likely to be present. Syntactical and/or spelling errors are likely to be present.	Answer makes some attempt to analyse the question, using mostly accurate factual material. However, it may well describe events rather than explain them, or explain them without much detail or depth. In multi-factor questions, the range of factors dealt with will be limited. It will be clearly written and have an obvious structure with paragraphs.

Level	Mark range	Mark scheme descriptor	What this means
4	19–24	Candidates offer an analytical response which relates well to the focus of the question and which shows some understanding of the key issues contained in it. The analysis will be supported by accurate factual material which will be mostly relevant to the question asked. The selection of material may lack balance in places. **Low Level 4: 19–20 marks** The qualities of Level 4 are displayed; material is less convincing in its range and depth. **Mid-Level 4: 21–22 marks** As per descriptor. **High Level 4: 23–24 marks** The qualities of Level 4 are securely displayed; material is convincing in range and depth consistent with Level 4. The answer will show some degree of direction and control but these attributes may not be sustained throughout the answer. The candidate will demonstrate the skills needed to produce convincing extended writing but there may be passages which lack clarity or coherence. The answer is likely to include some syntactical and/or spelling errors.	It is clear that the question has been understood and the answer is directed at the wording of the question using accurate support. Some attempt has been made to reach a judgement. However, the answer may not cover all the key points or the full time span of the question and may lose focus a little occasionally. It will be very well written and clearly structured.
5	25–30	Candidates offer an analytical response which directly addresses the focus of the question and which demonstrates explicit understanding of the key issues contained in it. It will be broadly balanced in its treatment of these key issues. The analysis will be supported by accurate, relevant and appropriately selected factual material which demonstrates some range and depth. **Low Level 5: 25–26 marks** The qualities of Level 5 are displayed; material is less convincing in its range and depth. **Mid-Level 5: 27–28 marks** As per descriptor. **High Level 5: 29–30 marks** The qualities of Level 5 are securely displayed; material is convincing in range and depth consistent with Level 5. The exposition will be controlled and the deployment logical. Some syntactical and/or spelling errors may be found but the writing will be coherent overall. The skills required to produce convincing extended writing will be in place.	The answer will tackle the question directly, addressing a wide range of relevant points and making links between them. As well as covering the full time period, it will show variations in the impact of different issues at different times. The relevance of points will be clearly explained and the focus on the question will be sustained. A strong concluding judgement will be reached. It will be well written and logically structured. However, even Level 5 answers are not perfect!

Preparing for the exam

Different people revise in different ways and by now you have been doing exams so long you may feel you have a successful revision strategy. However, History is a subject in which there is a lot to learn and some new strategies might be helpful. Always try to remember why you are likely to need particular areas of knowledge – what purpose is it likely to serve? This is not a knowledge-driven exam; you should use knowledge (evidence) to support a point in your argument, not just include it because you happen to have learned it!

Time charts

You could compile a huge time chart for the whole time period 1881–1924, or break it down according to the time periods covered by the four bullet points in the specification. Adapt the column headings to suit your focus. These are useful for consolidating your chronological knowledge, for making you analyse types of events and for showing links between political, socio-economic and foreign events. Here is an example of how you might start one.

Date	Political	Social/Economic	Foreign (if it influences domestic events)
1881	Start of reaction under Alexander III		
1891		Trans-Siberian Railway begun	
1893		Witte appointed Finance Minister	French alliance
1894	Accession of Nicholas II		

Biographical profiles of the key individuals

Download a photo of a key figure, for example Alexander III, Nicholas II, Lenin, Trotsky, Witte, Stolypin, Kerensky. Structure a biographical portrait, as in the example opposite (Stolypin). You could use the same categories, but obviously make amendments depending on, for example, whether the subject was defending or opposing the system in power at the time. These will help you focus on individuals, and make you think about what they did and why. You could easily convert your profiles into revision cards.

Pyotr Stolypin

Birth and background	1862 in Dresden; parents Russian gentry
Death	Assassinated 1911 – shot at Kiev Opera House
Jobs held (with dates)	Governor of Saratov province 1902–5
	Minister of Interior and Prime Minister 1906–11
Key things he did	1906–11 agricultural reforms – his 'wager on the strong'. Trying to create class of loyal, more prosperous peasantry who would defend status quo.
	Made it easier to leave *mir*, facilitated consolidation of strips.
	Encouraged Peasants' Land Bank to loan money.
	Encouraged eastwards migration to open up Siberia.
	Repression – mopped up rural unrest after 1905, hangings ('Stolypin's necktie'). Arrest of Vyborg signatories.
	Behind electoral law of 1907 which restricted franchise and made third and fourth Dumas amenable.
	Fell out with third Duma when he opposed extending the *zemstva* system.
Contribution to preserving the status quo	Mopped up aftermath of 1905 using repression.
	Stifled Duma criticism through new electoral law.
	Began to create what later became known as *kulak* class.
Why he is regarded as important to historians	Conservative reformer who might have preserved Tsarism, had he been trusted by Nicholas and lived longer.
	Mystery surrounding death illustrates Nicholas' unease with powerful ministers.
Other important factors	

Use essay planning frames

Planning frames will help you to practise how you would structure answers to previously set questions. Complete these in a disciplined way, using a format such as the one below.

Question	Type of question	Key words explained	
Introduction	**Line of argument**	**Range of factors to be considered**	
Main section paragraph 1	**Point**	**Supporting evidence**	**Relevance to the case**
Main section paragraphs 2 onwards (as required) should be continued in the same format as Main section paragraph 1			
Conclusion	**Judgement**	**Main reasons for the judgement**	

Revision checklist

Prepare a revision checklist, such as the one opposite. This checklist is only meant to be a starting point; you could go through your notes and prepare a much more thorough version by adding more detail. Only tick the *understood* column when you believe you have an aspect under control. Use the *areas of uncertainty* box to record things you need to do more work on.

People – the big names	Understood ✓	Acts of terror	Understood ✓
Alexander III		Assassination of Plehve	
Nicholas II		Bloody Sunday 1905	
Witte		Execution of royal family	
Stolypin		Suppression of Kronstadt rising 1921	
Trotsky			
Lenin			
Kerensky			
Other important people		**Organisations**	
Rasputin		The *Okhrana*	
Alexandra		The *Cheka*	
Pobedonostsev		The Orthodox Church	
Stolypin		The SRs	
		The SDs	
		Greens	
Reforms passed		**Concepts and ideas**	
Creation of Peasants' Land bank		Marxism	
Stolypin's land reforms		Bolshevism	
Decree on Nationalisation 1918		Dictatorship of the proletariat	
New Constitution 1918		Liberal	
New Constitution 1922		Autocracy	
Important places		**Key economic developments**	
Donets Basin		Getting on gold standard	
Putilov engineering works		Trans-Siberian Railway	
Lena goldfields		War Communism	
		NEP	
Areas of uncertainty			

And finally...

Do not memorise model answers. Read them and learn from them, but prepare for the unexpected because the same question is unlikely to crop up again. Understand and learn the topic thoroughly but answer the question in front of you, not the one you wish it had been!

Exemplar essays and commentaries

Question 1

'How far do you agree that the Bolsheviks' success in November 1917 was mainly due to the weaknesses of their rivals for power?' **[30 marks]**

The question is asking you to judge the extent to which the success of the Bolsheviks' coup was due to the weaknesses of any other groups who wanted power and how much it was due to their own positive attributes, or to other factors that helped the Bolshevik cause.

Grade C student answer

The Bolsheviks were successful in seizing power partly because the Provisional Government had serious weaknesses but also because the Bolsheviks themselves were strong enough to stage a coup. This was carried out in the second revolution of November. The first revolution was in March when Tsar Nicholas abdicated.

The Provisional Government was weak because it had no real right to be ruling Russia. It had taken over after the Tsar abdicated but it had not been elected to do this and its members came from the property-owning middle class – they didn't reflect the views of ordinary Russians. They delayed the elections because they thought it would be unfair to deny the vote to soldiers serving at the Front, but eventually they fixed the date for November. However, by this time it was too late and the Bolsheviks had already seized power.

Another weak point for the Provisional Government was that they failed to sort out the land problem, which resulted in the peasants taking land themselves. Many soldiers deserted from the army to take part in land seizures, especially after the new summer offensive went wrong and military morale reached an all-time low. If the Provisional Government had got out of the war, these weaknesses might have been avoided, but they wanted to keep getting the funding from their allies and they believed the war was about democracy against militarism so it was morally right to carry on. Unfortunately for them, most Russians disagreed and the war made the government unpopular.

However, the Bolsheviks also had strengths of their own which enabled them to succeed. Firstly Lenin was a ruthless and decisive leader. When he returned from exile and announced his April Theses, his promises of ☞

This is a direct start that addresses the question and establishes a basic context. However, it looks as though the range of material is going to be limited. A better start would indicate the range of weaknesses of the Provisional Government and of the other contributory factors.

This paragraph identifies a key weakness of the Provisional Government – its lack of legitimacy – and explains why their appeal was limited. It would be improved by some explanation of developments during the delay that cost them support.

This point links quite well with the previous one and is about an additional weakness that did undermine the Government. It loses focus a little in explaining the reasoning for continuing fighting. However, the final comment brings it back to the question of weakness. The factual material is accurate but lacks precision – there needs to be a sense that attitudes changed between March and November, and some reference to the Soviet's attempt to establish control over military loyalty.

This paragraph starts neatly and moves the answer on to examine Bolshevik strengths. Lenin's appeal is explained in a direct but general way, and there is some linkage back to the previous point about the war being unpopular. A better answer would strengthen the final sentence by linking desertions explicitly to land seizures and the government's failure to tackle redistribution seriously.

'peace, bread and land' proved popular with the peasants and workers. Most Russians were sick of the war and the food shortages that went with it and the peasants were anxious to get their hands on more land. When the war continued under the Provisional Government, soldiers deserted from the army in ever-growing numbers.

Lenin was also clever in building up the Soviet as an alternative to the government and he told the Bolsheviks to break off all cooperation with it. Gradually the Bolsheviks got to dominate the Soviet and, with the Provisional Government losing its early popularity, it became feasible for them to stage an armed coup without meeting too much opposition. Events such as the Kornilov Affair also helped the Bolsheviks regain popularity, which they seemed to have lost when their leaders had been jailed in the July Days Uprising.

A further paragraph on Lenin's positive impact. It actually covers two points: the manipulation of the Soviet and the exploitation of the Kornilov situation. Both are valid but neither is fully explained. There ought to be some explanation of the relationship between the Soviet and the Provisional Government, and the importance of Lenin's success in changing this. Also, there needs to be some explanation of why the Kornilov Affair turned out to be so helpful to the Bolsheviks.

The Bolsheviks were also helped by the Provisional Government's liberal approach to things so it was legal to speak out against them without any harassment from the secret police, which had been abolished. Also because they were the 'provisional' government no one expected them to stay long in power.

These are two valid and useful points that do link the two sides of the answer together but there is no supporting evidence provided. They would have had more impact if they had come earlier in the answer. Here, they look a bit like an afterthought.

In conclusion then, the Bolsheviks' success was down to a combination of errors and weaknesses shown by the Provisional Government and strengths shown by Lenin and the Bolsheviks, who realised what the ordinary Russian really wanted, which was an end to the fighting and a solution to the peasant land problem.

The conclusion does sum up the answer to the question, but is very brief. It ought to reassess the importance of really key pieces of evidence that have been discussed, such as the delays of key decisions by the Provisional Government and the leadership of Lenin. It does not quite reach a judgement.

The student addresses the question directly and maintains a focus on it almost throughout. It is clearly structured and well written, following a logical sequence of paragraphs. The points made are valid and the support provided is accurate.

However, both the range and depth are limited to some extent. In terms of range, the answer only examines the Provisional Government and the Bolsheviks – there is no recognition of other rivals.

Lack of depth is a bigger problem; for example, the Bolsheviks should have been examined beyond the influence of Lenin, the weaknesses of the Government should have been linked to Bolshevik strengths, and a sense of chronology was needed.

To improve the student must provide more supporting evidence that is linked explicitly to the question.

Overall, this answer achieves a low level 4 and would gain **20 marks**.

Excellent Grade A student answer

The Bolsheviks' success in their coup of November 1917 was due to a combination of the weaknesses of their potential rivals – the Socialist Revolutionaries, the Mensheviks and the Provisional Government – and of their own strengths and ability to exploit these weaknesses. While the other groups with the potential to hold power did definitely make mistakes, without the ruthlessness and clear vision of Lenin, aided by Trotsky, it is doubtful they would have succeeded.

The Provisional Government was the strongest of these 'rivals for power' as it had stepped into the vacuum left by Nicholas' abdication. Although it already had experience of government as the old Duma, it made its task harder by delaying vital decisions regarding elections and land redistribution. Until elections were held it had no legitimate claim to govern, but these weren't held until November. This was a crucial weakness because the leaders, Prince Lvov and then Kerensky, came from the privileged elite. Furthermore, they appeared to be half-hearted about redistributing land, merely setting up an inconclusive enquiry, which promised action after the elections. By the time the elections took place the Bolsheviks had staged their coup and the countryside had passed beyond the Provisional Government's control.

The decision to launch a new offensive and make continuing the war an essential part of the revolution was a further misjudgement made by the Provisional Government. It would have been quite possible to defend Russia's frontiers but scale down the level of military commitment, since the USA had entered the war in April 1917 and this would soon be requiring greater efforts by the Central Powers over in the West. However, once this new offensive ran into trouble, soldiers began to desert in large numbers and the government's grip on army loyalty began to slip away. Furthermore, continuing the war meant that the economy continued to experience the same problems as before – food shortages in the cities and rising inflation. The government had misjudged the level of popular enthusiasm for continuing the war.

Underpinning these weaknesses of the Provisional Government was their liberal approach to politics whereby censorship was replaced by free speech. Although this made them initially popular with those who had suffered from Tsarist repression, it also made it easier for critics to voice their opinions without fear of reprisals. Lenin would not have dared return ☞

This is a direct introduction that has addressed the question. The alternatives to the Bolsheviks have been identified and the line of argument made clear – that the coup was due to a combination of others' weaknesses and Bolshevik strengths, but that the latter were the most important.

This is the first of three paragraphs on the most significant obstacle to the Bolsheviks, the Provisional Government. Precise evidence is used to explain why the delays in holding elections and taking land redistribution seriously were damaging to their survival prospects. However, the final comment might have been strengthened by including some additional evidence to show how those not represented by this 'privileged elite' had lost confidence in the Provisional Government by November and were taking matters into their own hands.

This point has been made well and there is a useful contextual comment about the war, which highlights the weakness of the government on this issue. It would have been even better to explain that, since continuing the war was not widely popular, continued economic suffering would soon cause opposition to grow.

This is an important general point about the Provisional Government, which has been linked to the previous points at the end of the paragraph.

under the Tsarist regime nor would the Marxists in general have been able to stir up trouble and produce such quantities of critical propaganda. The Petrograd Soviet, which the Bolsheviks made their focal point, would simply not have been allowed to exist. The weaknesses which the Provisional Government had shown regarding legitimacy, land reform and the war were freely exploited by their enemies.

Although both the Socialist Revolutionaries and the Mensheviks offered alternatives to the Provisional Government, they were seriously handicapped by indecision over how much to collaborate with it. Chernov returned from exile to lead the Socialist Revolutionaries, but he couldn't get them to agree. Theoretically, the extent of their support from the peasantry (80% of the population) ought to have been a great advantage but, in reality, the peasants were impossible to organise coherently since they thought mainly of local grievances or short-term gains. The Mensheviks, too, differed over the question of collaboration, but their decision to continue doing this made it easy for the Bolsheviks to portray them as friends of the bourgeoisie. They had a foothold in the Soviet initially, but lost the advantage that this gave them. Fundamentally, the Mensheviks lacked the urgency of their Bolshevik rivals, since they were prepared to see the March Revolution as the bourgeois revolution, which had to be given time to fail before the mass working-class revolution could be expected. For them, November was much too soon. The actions of the Socialist Revolutionaries and Mensheviks contributed to the erosion of the Provisional Government's power, but neither offered a realistic alternative government.

Unlike the Mensheviks, the Bolshevik leadership was much more decisive. Lenin succeeded in transmitting his urgency to seize power over to his Bolshevik colleagues, persuading them to break off all links with the Provisional Government and concentrate instead on taking over the Petrograd Soviet. This made it harder for the government to command the loyalty of the workers and soldiers, emphasising the problems caused by their lack of legitimacy. Once he had persuaded the Central Committee to agree to a coup in November, the Bolsheviks could seize power before the scheduled elections took place. Trotsky also played a key part by organising the details of the coup through the Military Revolutionary Committee and ensuring that any resistance was dealt with efficiently. The fact that the Socialist Revolutionaries then won the most seats in ☞

This is an important paragraph that shows wider knowledge – that the struggle was not simply between the Bolsheviks and the Provisional Government. It starts by linking back to the wording of the question and then provides clear evidence about the internal problems handicapping both the Socialist Revolutionaries and Mensheviks. Specialist vocabulary has been used with confidence: bourgeoisie, March Revolution. The final point makes it clear that, though relevant to the government's difficulties, neither of these groups posed a sufficiently serious threat to them.

This paragraph is vital to the argument and makes it clear why leadership (mainly, but not entirely, from Lenin) was such a powerful force. The contrast with the Menshevik approach is made at the start. There is a clear link back to the legitimacy problem of the government. It might have been strengthened with some comment about Lenin's personal qualities, for example, his ruthlessness in closing down the Assembly, which contrasted with the liberal approach shown by the Provisional Government's leaders.

these elections shows just how important Lenin's sense of timing was, since a coup after this would have been hard to justify but, with power in his hands already, Lenin was not afraid to simply close down the new assembly. This strong leadership from Lenin and Trotsky contrasted with the liberal approach of the Provisional Government and the indecision of the Socialist Revolutionaries and Mensheviks.

However, several of the incidents that contributed to the Bolsheviks' success were only possible because of the weaknesses of their rivals, so it is a combination of the two that accounts for their eventual success in November. The Provisional Government, as well as making the crucial delays to elections and land issues, also mishandled the Kornilov coup in such a way that it played into the Bolsheviks' hands. Having been discredited as traitors in the July Days, the Bolsheviks were released from prison and could pose as guardians of Russia thanks to Kerensky's misreading of the threat posed by General Kornilov.

This is a really useful paragraph because it shows the links between the Provisional Government's mistakes and Bolshevik success. It also brings in the July Days and Kornilov Affair, neither of which had been referred to before, so a fuller chronological range is being covered.

In conclusion then, it seems that the Bolsheviks' main rival for power, the Provisional Government, lost control of the country because of its various weaknesses and errors, but it was only the Bolsheviks who proved capable of exploiting these opportunities. The Socialist Revolutionaries were divided, as were the Mensheviks, who also took a longer-term view of revolution. Taking advantage of the freedom to organise opposition, Lenin was able to return to Petrograd and organise the Bolsheviks to stage a successful coup in November. He could claim that the Bolsheviks were the only group untainted by collaboration with the Provisional Government. It was therefore a combination of others' weaknesses and Bolsheviks' strengths that accounted for the coup – the door to power had been left open, but the Bolsheviks turned out to be the only group capable of pushing through it. They did so decisively in November 1917.

The conclusion summarises the argument quite concisely, reviewing main weaknesses of the Provisional Government, Socialist Revolutionaries and Mensheviks and some key Bolshevik strengths. The argument has therefore been clarified and an overall judgement reached.

This is a very strong response. The question is tackled directly and the focus has been secured by the concluding sentence in each paragraph. Each point has been presented in an analytical way, with no irrelevant material. Range and depth are both thorough, facts have been selected discriminatingly and there is appropriate use of specialist vocabulary.

Overall, this answer achieves a high level 4 and would gain **29 marks**.

Question 2

'To what extent did the Russian economy change between 1881 and 1914?'
[30 marks]

The question is asking you to judge the amount of change in the economy over a fixed period of time. As well as identifying those areas of the economy that changed a significant amount, you will also need to point out where less change occurred. Good answers will show awareness that the pace of change was not constant and will make clear the criteria by which change can be judged (for example, industrial and agricultural output, changes in the way things were organised and financed). You will need to break down 'economy' into key components, notably industry and agriculture, but also cover the issue of how things were financed. Beware of switching the focus to the reasons why it changed – this can be valuable in the correct context but is not what the question is asking for.

Borderline Grade C/D student answer

The Russian economy underwent enormous growth in this period, although it was still not on a par with the economies of Britain or Germany by 1914. Most of the growth was kick-started by Witte, who began the 'great spurt' in the 1890s, but it is debatable whether Russia was really modernised enough by 1914 to be seen as a Great Power, and the industrial growth that occurred also brought significant social problems in the cities. There was also modernisation in agriculture but this was slower than that in industry.

The person most associated with changing the economy was Sergei Witte, the Finance Minister during 1892–1903. However, before him there was Bunge, who had reduced the taxes peasants had to pay, and then Vyshnegradsky, who had taxed them as much as possible to raise more revenue. Neither of these two was very successful in changing the economy but Witte put Russia on the gold standard and persuaded foreign businessmen to invest in Russia. The economy began to advance rapidly in the 1890s and Witte's big rail scheme, the Trans-Siberian line, helped the economy to grow because it opened up Siberia to trade and won great prestige for Russia as an equivalent of the railroads opening up the American West.

France and Belgium invested huge amounts in Russia, seeing the profits to be made by helping to exploit its resources. Russia massively increased its coal production and even began to build oil wells as the economy developed. The urban areas grew as peasants flooded in to work in ☞

This introduction sets economic change in a simple context but does not focus carefully on the wording of the question. Instead it comments on two linked, but not directly relevant, side issues: comparison with other Great Powers and the growth of social problems.

This paragraph and the next provide some accurate and relevant information about economic and industrial change, but have been put together in a fragmentary way and lack any knowledge of regional variations or any statistical comments.

The criteria that will be used for judging change have not been identified and the points have not been adequately explained; for example, it is not clear why the use of foreign investment was so important – there is no recognition that Russia lacked a commercial class of investors of its own.

This paragraph gets sidetracked into the social side effects of industrialisation. To improve, the section should be finished off with an overall judgement on how much change had occurred since 1881.

the expanding factories of Moscow and St Petersburg. However, these changes weren't without their problems and as the cities grew bigger so did the social problems in them. One of the main reasons behind the 1905 revolution was the terrible living and working conditions, which Father Gapon was demonstrating against on Bloody Sunday.

It was Alexander II who realised that the economy needed to be improved, after he lost the Crimean War, and he immediately freed the serfs from ownership by the landowners. However, agriculture remained in a backward condition even after this and the peasants still preferred strip-farming and using traditional methods. Russia sold much of the grain abroad but still wasn't feeding the people at home and there were serious famines on several occasions due to this. The peasants resented paying high taxes and frequently took part in uprisings or jacqueries against rich landowners. After this discontent peaked in 1905, Stolypin tried to reform agriculture by creating a richer class of peasant who would be on the government's side in future.

This paragraph and the next deal with agriculture. The first is a general description of the state of agriculture at the start of the period, with some explanation of why it was in a backward condition and why changes speeded up. This is useful context, but not actually what the question is asking.

The main change he introduced made it possible for peasants to leave the *mir* and farm independently. They could borrow more easily from the banks and invest in new machinery or new methods if they wished. Many even migrated east to Siberia and began to exploit the farming potential there. Opinions vary on how much Stolypin actually changed things, but grain production did go up significantly before the war and many peasants did free themselves from the control of the *mir* and used bank loans to buy up more land and farm it more effectively. Lenin even thought that there was less chance of a revolution because a substantial section of the peasantry were becoming prosperous and content due to these changes, which suggests they must have had considerable impact.

Here the student discusses the post-1905 changes to agriculture but the paragraph lacks depth of knowledge on the impact of the land reforms. The evidence is potentially useful but generalised as it stands.

In conclusion, Russia's economy did change a lot and became much more modern and industrialised between 1881 and 1914. However, Russia was still not an economic Great Power on the same level as Germany or the UK and also by modernising the economy so rapidly they had helped cause the Revolution of 1905. Most of the changes were thanks to the policies of Witte who got foreign money invested in Russian industry and launched the 'great spurt' of industrial growth, and Stolypin who launched his wager on the strong. By 1914 Russia was producing much greater quantities of industrial goods and grain than in 1881; however, the economic changes can't have been that great overall or Russia would have performed better than she did in the First World War.

The conclusion reaches a judgement of sorts but it has been based on a limited amount of evidence and the focus here drifts again into the issue of whether Russia was as economically developed as other Great Powers, which is not the question set. The final sentence looks like an afterthought and needs some explanation. ☞

What prevents this from being an effective assessment is the failure to set out clearly how the extent of change can be judged – this is left implicit.

The range of evidence is limited on both industrial and agricultural change, with only passing references to how changes were financed. There is some analysis, but there are limitations in terms of range and depth, and the focus occasionally strays off the question.

Overall, this answer achieves a level 3 and would gain **16 marks**.

Grade A student answer

The period between 1881 and 1914 saw the Russian economy undergo significant development in terms of industrialisation and financial investment. Agriculture, while lagging behind, was also changing as the stranglehold on progress exerted by the *mir* was relaxed. Russia may not have had a modern economy on a par with Britain or Germany in 1914, but it had made genuine progress since 1881, in terms of sheer output of industrial goods, the development of factories and the efforts being made by the state to attract outside investment. However, although judgement of the extent of change can partly be based on statistical evidence, it isn't easy to reach a definite overall answer because the Marxists, who were in power after 1917, played down the economic progress made under the Tsars in order to exaggerate their own achievements.

> The introduction gives an overview and indicates how the answer will be structured. It has been made clear that Communist propaganda makes an accurate judgement more difficult – so matters of interpretation are being addressed. It also indicates the key criteria by which change might be judged.

In terms of industry, Russia had changed dramatically by 1914. In 1881 there were some factories, mainly producing textiles in St Petersburg and Moscow, and iron was being produced in the Urals. However, Russia had not yet experienced an industrial revolution. Moreover the communications system was undeveloped which, due to the sheer size of Russia, was a major limiting factor. Further constraints were imposed by the lack of a proper banking system and the absence of a middle class with capital to invest in new developments.

> This brief section is valid because it establishes the situation at the start before the changes began.

However, Russia began to industrialise seriously in the 1890s, while Witte was Finance Minister. Although this didn't continue uninterrupted until 1914 (there was a recession from about 1900 to 1903) by the time of the outbreak of the war Russia had nearly 25 000 factories, many of which were extremely large, employing thousands of workers (for example, the Putilov engineering works in St Petersburg). Moreover, large-scale coal production was taking place in the Ukraine and the oil industry had transformed Baku on the ☞

> This paragraph sums up the extent of industrial change by 1914, using selected statistics. It shows a grasp of the geographical variations in the changes and that change was not constant over the whole period. The vocabulary helps convey the changes: 'however' 'moreover' 'transformed' and 'undeniable'.

Caspian Sea, as well as metal and textiles developing significantly elsewhere. Peasants had poured in to the big cities from the countryside to work in the expanding factories to such an extent that both Moscow and St Petersburg had more than doubled their populations since 1881, each having about two million inhabitants. Over the whole period the value of Russia's annual industrial output had increased fourfold so there had been undeniable change in the productive capacity of industry and the working lives of the urban population.

Witte focused on developing the railway system, using foreign investment which poured in once Russia was on the gold standard in 1897. By 1914 Russia had 70 000 kilometres of railway, compared to a mere 20 000 in 1881. Significant investment was also put into the mines, where raw materials were produced, and the factories that processed them. A deliberate policy of state capitalism, whereby the capital was directed where needed by the government, became the accepted way things were done, and again this made change happen more quickly than in the past when investment decisions were left very much to individuals.

However, there were of course limitations in this picture of industrial expansion. There may have been three million industrial workers by 1914, but this was still a tiny percentage of the total population, which remained overwhelmingly peasant (80%). In addition there remained vast untapped economic resources in Siberia and more remote regions and, although the rail system had made transport of goods easier and cheaper, the Trans-Siberian line was still incomplete in 1914 and is regarded more as a symbolic sign of Russia's possibilities than a practical asset. While foreign investment and expertise certainly did change things, the reliance on this meant the growth would be fragile until a strong Russian commercial class developed, and this showed little sign of happening. Also the rate of change was patchy, with little if any progress occurring in the recession of 1900–03, and then came the war against Japan and the turmoil of the 1905 revolution, which further disrupted economic progress. Change still depended largely on the efforts of forceful Finance Ministers; however, Nicholas II distrusted such people and once Witte resigned in 1906 there was less direction from above, so things didn't develop as fast as they might have done towards the end of the period. ☞

This is the third of three paragraphs providing evidence of industrial change, this time focusing on how changes were financed.

This paragraph is essential in balancing the answer, as it shows areas where change was either limited or barely occurred. Accurate evidence regarding communications, transport, diversion of resources into war and political misjudgements by the Tsar are all used to show significant elements of continuity. A final sentence judging the overall balance between change and continuity in industry would have strengthened it.

In contrast, agriculture changed less noticeably than industry over the period, and in fact the key change here was the emancipation of the serfs, which had happened back in 1861. However, emancipation had certainly not created a thriving agricultural economy by 1881 for a whole range of reasons; there was much northerly land unsuited to arable or livestock farming and in the most fertile crop growing areas, the Black Earth regions of European Russia, there was a shortage of land to go round. Those peasants who borrowed to buy more land were saddled with serious levels of debt, as were the freed serfs whose redemption payments lasted 49 years. The peasantry held deeply conservative attitudes, persisting in strip-farming and out-of-date methods, so crop yields were much lower than they might have been.

This section summarises the position in agriculture at the start of the period, emphasising the factors holding back change.

By 1914 however, agriculture was certainly changing as a result of Stolypin's land reforms, which began in response to the unrest of 1905. Stolypin had lifted some of the tax burdens on the peasantry by ending redemption payments several years early and had pushed through legislation that enabled peasants to leave the *mir* and consolidate their strips into more efficient units. He had also expanded the resources of the Land Bank, which offered low-interest loans to enable peasants to buy more land or to migrate eastwards and settle in Siberia, which was being opened up by the rail system. The statistics do suggest significant changes had occurred as a result, for example 20% of the peasants had left the *mir* by 1916.

This compares the state of agriculture in 1914 with that of 1881, using precise factual evidence to show what changed and when. The section is shorter than that on industry because there was less change going on.

Nevertheless, it does seem clear that agriculture was not changing as quickly as industry despite the reforms of Stolypin, for example the strip system was still the norm in 1914. While historians agree that progress was being made in changing agriculture, they disagree on how far this had got by 1914 and many argue that Stolypin's reforms alone would not have been enough to sustain Russia in the future.

This section shows the limitations of the agricultural changes. It could have been strengthened by some comments on the assassination of Stolypin and the possibility that the Tsar had already lost interest in his approach – this could have been used to put more emphasis on the failure to change agriculture more effectively.

Finally it is worth examining how changes were financed in order to reach an overall judgement on the extent of change. In 1881 more revenue came from taxing the population than in 1914, but the dangers of subjecting the peasantry to excessive taxation demands had become all too obvious when they rose up in 1905. By 1914, the emphasis had shifted more to borrowing from abroad and attracting foreign investment in developing the Russian economy. The key element that ☞

This section contains a bit of overlap with the industrial growth section, but even exam essays attaining a high grade are rarely perfect and the changes in how Russia's economic development was financed are important.

changed in finance then was the switch in raising revenue from mainly internal to external sources, accompanied by the gradual development of a suitable banking system.

In conclusion, it is fair to say that the Russian economy in 1914 was significantly different to that of 1881, particularly in terms of industrial development. Russia had experienced an industrial revolution in which existing towns had grown into cities, it was accessing its raw materials (coal, iron ore and oil) on a scale far beyond that of 1881 and was mass-producing manufactured goods in important quantities. Clearly the progress was patchy in terms of geography (European Russia, the Ukraine and the Caspian seeing the fastest changes) and in terms of time, with the fastest bursts coming in 1893–99 and 1908–14. Unfavourable comparisons with western European countries don't mean that Russia itself wasn't changing extensively. In terms of agriculture however, the changes were slower and less dramatic, and the fact that Russia was overwhelmingly a peasant society does mean that the slow pace of change in this sector of the economy was a crucial factor limiting the extent of change. Change was also clear in the way economic developments were financed, with the reliance on western investment becoming well established from the 1890s onwards. However, by the time that war broke out in 1914, it is safe to say that Russia had experienced remarkable levels of economic change and had avoided becoming what Witte allegedly feared, a 'European China' that was a treated like a colony by the great powers.

A judgement has been reached despite the varied nature of the evidence that has been assessed. The key changes have been reiterated and the extent of change summarised neatly.

The student sustains a focus on comparing the economy of 1914 with that of 1881 and while there is some descriptive material relating to the state of the economy, this has been used to support statements about change or continuity – it is not provided for its own sake.

The factual support is precise. The structure is clear and economic activity has been broken down into logical areas of industry, agriculture and finance. A final judgement has been reached, based on the evidence provided.

However, it would have been higher in the level if it had made more frequent and explicit references to the key criteria for judging extent of change. These were hinted at in the introduction, but they should be central to the judgement and referred to at the end of each paragraph. The length of the answer also detracts a little from the sharpness of the argument.

Overall, this answer achieves a level 5 and would gain **25 marks**.

Question 3

'Why, despite their limited level of support in 1917, were the Bolsheviks still in power in 1924?' **[30 marks]**

This 'why' question is asking you not only to explain the reasons why the Bolsheviks were still in power by 1924, but also to discuss weaknesses in their power base that they had to address or overcome.

Grade C student answer

When the Bolsheviks staged their coup in November 1917 they had little popular support, as they were only an urban workers' party. This could have been a serious limitation on their efforts to stay in control, but they succeeded in fighting off the White challenge in the Civil War and by 1924 their power was reasonably secure. The main reasons for their success in consolidating power were the leadership shown by Lenin and Trotsky and the fact that they won the Civil War.

> This is a clear introduction that addresses the question, but the range of reasons identified is limited to two, so it is lacking range.

Lenin was the undisputed leader of the Bolsheviks and he made sure that key tactical decisions were taken. For example, one main reason why the Provisional Government had failed was that it had carried on fighting the First World War, so Lenin made sure that Russia left the war by agreeing to the Treaty of Brest-Litovsk. This helped to make the Bolsheviks more popular.

> This is a good point but it has not been fully explained. The benefits for the Bolsheviks of leaving the war need to be given. The final sentence is too general – it needs to specify with whom it was popular.

Another key decision was to close the Constituent Assembly because the Bolsheviks had only won a small number of seats in the elections and they wouldn't have been able to get their policies passed though parliament. They weren't concerned about democracy and enforced their ideas using the Cheka and Red Army against any opposition. Lenin was behind both these decisions and Trotsky was head of the Red Army, so their leadership helped enforce Bolshevik control.

> Again this is a valid point, and it is clear the question has been understood because it is being addressed directly. However, again there is little explanation of how these moves actually helped the Bolsheviks. More detailed support is also needed about who the opposition was and what the *Cheka* did.

The decision to replace War Communism with the New Economic Policy (NEP) was another important decision that Lenin took that helped the Bolsheviks stay in power. War Communism, especially grain requisitioning, was really unpopular with the peasants who were growing as little food as possible, contributing to a serious famine and lack of food in the cities. Lenin realised that peasants would only grow more if they were allowed to make a profit, so he authorised the reintroduction of some capitalist practices in the countryside and brought ☞

> This is a more effective paragraph because the relevance of the decision to bring in NEP has been explained. There ought to be a date provided to show how the situation was changing during this period.

> The idea of summing up the importance of Lenin's leadership is good, but the answer needs to explain why it mattered and provide more precise detail about the roles played by Lenin and Trotsky, and why feeding the cities was vital to the success of the Red Army.

in NEP. This was unpopular with the left wing of the party who thought it was too much like capitalism, but Lenin saw that it was necessary to get food production up again and said it would only be for a few years until the economy got on its feet. These decisions by Lenin, aided by Trotsky, were therefore very important in increasing the Bolsheviks' control of Russia.

However, the main reason why the Bolsheviks were able to stay in power was because they defeated the Whites in the Civil War which broke out between 1919 and 1921. Trotsky transformed the Red Army into a brutal and disciplined force. The Whites were seriously divided and never worked together as a team; Denikin in the south, Yudenich in the west and Kolchak in the east never collaborated, which allowed Trotsky to deal with them one at a time. Also the allied help that the Whites received was soon withdrawn. The Reds had some significant advantages that combined to help them win, particularly their control of the rail system and the fact that most of Russia's industries happened to be situated in the central areas that the Reds controlled.

This paragraph on the Bolsheviks' victory in the Civil War contains much accurate material about the relative strengths and weaknesses of the combatants. The point in the next paragraph about peasant support is valid but a little generalised. It would be worth explaining that it was the Bolshevik land decree of 1918 that authorised the land redistribution. Opportunities to link what is good knowledge to the wording of the question have not been taken.

Although the peasants weren't enthusiastic about Communism, they thought they would be worse off if the Whites won because the landowners would get their land back. This meant that the peasants went along with what the Reds wanted most of the time, although they hated grain requisitioning and often rebelled against this.

Overall the Bolsheviks managed to stay in power and increase their control from Petrograd to the whole of Russia because Lenin, along with Trotsky, was an outstanding leader who could impose his will on the Bolsheviks. However, if they hadn't succeeded in defeating the White forces in the Civil War, even Lenin's leadership wouldn't have been enough to keep them in power so in the end it was the victory in the Civil War that was crucial.

The conclusion sums up the argument that has been presented and reaches a judgement, but this has been based on a limited number of points.

The student has addressed the question in a relatively focussed way, and ensured that their answer is logically constructed , clearly written and reaches judgement.

However, the range of reasons presented is limited and the paragraphs on leadership are poorly developed. Only passing reference is made to popular support - this is referred to in the question so must be more specifically addressed. A higher mark could be achieved by making clear how the Bolsheviks succeeded in addressing the initial problems and those that developed later during the period.

Overall, this answer achieves a low level 4 and would gain **19 marks**.

Grade A student answer

Support for the Bolsheviks was limited to sections of the urban working class in the big cities, so in terms of Russia as a whole their support certainly was seriously limited. However, despite this handicap they had tightened their grip by 1924, for three main reasons. Firstly they made pragmatic and ruthless decisions quickly to enable them to survive the most urgent crises; secondly they set up a centralised state, which made it easier to take such decisions; thirdly, but most importantly, they had the monopoly of the means of enforcing terror and were not afraid to use these means ruthlessly against all potential opponents. These approaches helped the Bolsheviks overcome the immediate problems of the First World War and their limited appeal, and then the longer-term problems caused by economic instability and the outbreak of Civil War as political opposition came into the open.

It is impossible to know exactly how much support the Bolsheviks really had in November 1917. While the Bolsheviks had got a majority on the Petrograd Soviet by November, in the Constituent Assembly elections they only got 24% of the popular vote, compared to 41% for the Socialist Revolutionaries. This is hardly surprising since 80% of Russians were peasants in 1917 and the Bolsheviks were an urban working-class group. However, because they were prepared to take key pragmatic decisions, even if they went against their ideology, they managed to overcome the limitations caused by the narrow base of their initial support.

To stay in power the Bolsheviks needed to stifle political opposition straight away, so press censorship was immediately introduced and the new Constituent Assembly was closed down as soon as it was obvious the Socialist Revolutionaries had won a majority. However, by the time it met in January 1918 the Bolsheviks had already set up the Sovnarkom (Council of People's Commissars), a brand new body composed entirely of Bolsheviks, that had begun to issue decrees to give themselves breathing space. The land decree bought off the peasants by giving them the right to carry on seizing it themselves, the nationalisation decrees gave factory workers the right to control their workplaces and the national minorities were given self-determination. All these measures went further than the Bolsheviks wanted but for the time being they had won at least ☞

This is a clear introduction, which identifies three reasons for Bolshevik continuation in power and shows understanding of the level of support they had in 1917. It also addresses the nature of the problems the Bolsheviks would have to overcome in order to stay in power.

This is an essential section explaining the difficulty of quantifying Bolshevik support – which shows a sense of perspective – and indicating the consequence of this lack of support.

This paragraph contains detailed and accurate factual evidence about important changes introduced by the Bolsheviks in the first few weeks after the coup. Level 5 answers are expected to show awareness of the variation in the impact of factors at different points in time, which this paragraph does at the start. It also shows understanding that some changes were concessions that they did not necessarily believe in and that problems were being stored up for the future. The final sentence makes the point explicitly relevant to the question – it is worth remembering that in long paragraphs like this, explanation of relevance at the end is even more important than ever.

the temporary goodwill of huge parts of the population, which helped to expand their support base into the countryside and out to the fringes of the empire.

In a similar vein, Lenin insisted on accepting the German peace terms at Brest-Litovsk, even though they involved sacrificing hugely valuable swathes of land. All these decisions can be seen as necessary strategic moves that helped keep the Bolsheviks in power in the early months after the coup, whether they fitted in with Communist ideology or not.

> This could have been part of the previous paragraph as it is another important piece of evidence about the compromises Lenin made and the final remark is useful as it summarises the overall purpose of the concessions. It also links back to the economic problems identified in the introduction.

The Bolsheviks continued to place the practical realities of staying in power above their ideological preferences after 1918. In 1921 when the New Economic Policy, along with its capitalist elements, was brought in to replace the grain requisitioning of War Communism. With the Civil War won, and public opposition to the sufferings of War Communism reaching dangerous levels in the the Kronstadt rebellion, the Bolshevik leaders felt obliged to make new concessions to get the peasants producing food again – even if they involved restoring the profit motive in the countryside. Without taking these bold but ideologically contradictory steps it is doubtful if the Bolsheviks would have survived beyond 1921.

> This is a vital part of the argument because it shows that strategic decision-making was not just something the Bolsheviks were forced into at the outset, when the sheer number of problems could have swamped them, but a tactic they continued to employ. It rounds off the first of the reasons identified in the introduction.

However, the Bolsheviks would not have been able to take these decisive measures if they had not acted quickly to set up a centralised state where power was restricted to an inner circle of leaders. With no blueprint for running the country at the time of the coup, the Bolsheviks improvised quickly by setting up the Sovnarkom, a new state body, which issued the early decrees, and by closing the new Assembly. The Sovnarkom was soon overtaken in importance by the Politburo, a small party committee chaired by Lenin, while the ban on factions in 1921 ensured that opinions inside the party conformed to the leader's wishes. In this way, both party and state were placed under central control and quick decisions could be taken without time being taken up in consultation. Russia became a one-party state and press censorship of other political viewpoints reinforced Bolshevik control of public opinion. Organising decision-making in this way and narrowing down the numbers of those involved in making policy meant the Bolsheviks could act quickly and decisively to take whatever steps were necessary to ensure their survival. ☞

> The second reason under discussion is linked neatly to the first. Clear but not excessively detailed support is provided to explain the way power was centralised and that the party rather than the state became dominant. It would be worth pointing out that the threat of expulsion from the party helped reinforce party solidarity, since membership was a privilege worth having. Also, it would be worth including details of the new Constitution that enabled the Bolsheviks to survive – notably its federal nature, which bought off the national minority groups. Again the final comment is linked to the issues raised in the question.

However, the Bolsheviks would still have struggled to extend their control if they had not exercised sole control of the forces of repression and terror, through the Red Army and the Cheka. It was the Red Army that closed down the Constituent Assembly in January 1918 and Trotsky converted it into an effective, reasonably professional force. The Bolsheviks needed an effective army because political opposition to them soon materialised in the Civil War of 1918. If the Red Army hadn't defeated the various White armies in this Civil War then obviously the Bolsheviks could not have stayed in power, so its strength was vital to their success. Both sides treated the peasants badly but the Reds seemed the lesser of two evils, since at least a Red victory was less likely to deprive them of their newly acquired land – even if they had to endure grain requisitioning in the short term. Once the war was effectively won, the Red Army continued to keep order, crushing the Kronstadt rebels in 1921.

The other means of enforcing terror was through the Cheka, the Bolshevik secret police set up immediately after the coup, which immediately set about rounding up Kadet, Socialist Revolutionary and Menshevik leaders. The assassination attempt on Lenin in 1918 gave them the excuse to intensify their efforts and start the period known as the Red Terror. The royal family was shot and many thousands of people killed, as workers were encouraged to wage class war on the middle classes. Re-named the GPU, they continued to grow under the New Economic Policy and the fear engendered by their brutality and arbitrary arrests prevented organised opposition to the Bolsheviks. The Church was a particular target because of the alternative ideology it offered and the hold it already had over people. This monopoly of terror that the Bolsheviks possessed was the key factor enabling them to tighten their grip on power. Their reliance on such extensive terror reflected the limited nature of their initial support and the creation of a climate of fear greater than that under the Okhrana shows how successful the approach was in overcoming this.

In conclusion, the Bolsheviks extended their power from a fragile foothold in 1917 to a reasonably secure base by 1924, through these three interconnected reasons, and the initial lack of widespread public support did not handicap them too greatly. Over the period as a whole the most important reason why the Bolsheviks ☞

This section on the role of the Red Army as the enforcers of Bolshevik policy is detailed and accurate and the point of the paragraph is made clear at the outset. It explains reasons why the Red Army was both necessary (a link back to the introduction where problems facing the Bolsheviks are identified) and successful, without going into excessive detail about the military events of the Civil War. It also deals with the Red Army's role before and after the war. The final comment about Kronstadt is a telling one to illustrate the extent of Bolshevik ruthlessness. The focus is being sustained on the question.

The importance of the *Cheka* as the other arm of Bolshevik terror is clearly made and supported here. The fact that only the Bolsheviks possessed such means is important and the reference to the successful use of terror shows that the issues raised by the question are being addressed.

The conclusion draws the argument together and reiterates the links between the relevant factors. It also refers back to the issue of lack of popular support, which was specified in the question and finishes with a relevant comment about its extent by 1924. It is therefore a strong concluding judgement.

stayed in power was that it was only they who possessed the means to terrorise the rest of the population effectively. Lenin, who nearly always got his way, was opportunistic and made tactical concessions in order to win time to establish better control, and because they had centralised the state it was possible to take such decisions quickly. They used terror to enforce these decisions, which prevented any rival group getting strong enough to threaten them. By 1924, even if the older generation were not all passionate Bolsheviks, far more of them were reconciled to Bolshevik rule and many had tried to adapt their lives to it by applying for party membership so their appeal had broadened beyond its narrow beginnings.

The student has tackled the question directly and organised their answer into a clear structure where the reasons follow on logically and are clearly linked together. Normally it is advisable to deal with the main point in the argument first of all, but in this case the logical progression of the answer justifies addressing it last. Within the three reasons addressed a wide range of relevant sub-points are dealt with, and the full time period of 1917– 24 is covered.

The key issues have been understood and a wide range of accurate and appropriately detailed evidence has been used to support the points.

Focus on the question is sustained throughout and reinforced by the comments at the end of the main sections. The issue of Bolshevik popularity as a constraint has also been given adequate attention, as have the problems that the Bolsheviks had to overcome.

Specialist vocabulary has been used confidently and the answer as a whole is coherently expressed.

Overall, this answer achieves a level 5 and would gain **28 marks**.

Question 4

*'How accurate is it to say that the most important result of the 1905
Revolution was the creation of the Duma or national parliament?'* **[30 marks]**

This question requires knowledge of the results of the 1905 Revolution
and a judgement of whether the most important result was the creation
of a Duma (the stated consequence) or other outcomes. At least two other
consequences should be considered.

Grade C student answer

The 1905 Revolution began with the Bloody Sunday
massacre and continued until the Moscow uprising
was crushed in December, by which time the Tsar had
recovered his hold on power. It had several important
results, the most significant of which was the setting up
of the Duma.

The Duma was important because it was the first time
there had been a national elected parliament in Russia.
However, it lacked any real power because in the
Fundamental Law it said the Tsar could dissolve it for
any reason and rule without it if he wanted to. In fact
he did dissolve the first two Dumas very quickly when
they criticised him, but he never ruled for long without
it because he wanted to look democratic to the outside
world, especially the French who were lending large
sums of money to Nicholas. After the second Duma he
changed the electoral system so fewer people could
vote and Dumas after this didn't achieve very much.
Some liberals, the Octobrists, liked the Duma while the
Kadets complained bitterly about the restrictions. It was
still going in 1914 but Nicholas soon suspended it when
the war broke out, so overall the Duma wasn't such an
important result as it seemed it would be in 1906.

Another important set of changes was Stolypin's
reforms, which lasted from 1906 until his assassination
in 1911. He was unpopular because he was so tough on
the opposition that still lingered on after 1905, having
hundreds of troublemakers executed, but he also brought
in important land reforms that helped the peasants. They
no longer had to pay the redemption payments which
they had been saddled with since 1861, and they could
buy up more land if they wanted to. The Peasants' Land
Bank lent them the money to do this at low interest
rates and they were also encouraged to move out to
develop Siberia where there was more available ☞

The first sentence is accurate but it does not directly
address the question. The importance of the stated
consequence is then confirmed but there is no
indication given of other consequences, or of why the
creation of the Duma was so important.

This section starts well with a directly relevant
comment but then the importance of the Duma is not
properly explained: there needs to be some discussion
of whether autocracy was actually changing in reality,
or whether the changes were merely a façade. The
comments about why Nicholas kept the Dumas going
are valid but they are not made relevant.

There is quite a lot that could be added to improve
the paragraph; for example:

- detail about how the electoral system was altered
  and why this is significant
- recognition of the reforms the later Dumas
  passed.

The final comment about 1914 could easily have
been made stronger by explaining that the speed
with which Nicholas sidelined the Duma in wartime
emphasises how little he actually valued it, although
some attempt has been made to sum up the point at
the end. There is not any recognition of the reforms
the later Dumas passed.

land. Many peasants were able to leave the old fashioned *mir* and use more modern farming techniques. Grain yields began to improve and Russia was able to sell huge amounts abroad. These reforms therefore were another important result of 1905.

To sum up, the Duma was the most important result of the 1905 Revolution because some people see it as Russia's first step towards democracy. However, others see it as mere 'window dressing' to disguise the continuing autocracy behind the scenes. It also made Stolypin bring in the peasant land reforms so that there wouldn't be a future peasant revolution. However, neither of these results was really that important because, once the war broke out in 1914, the Tsar focused all his attention on that – the Duma was suspended and the land reforms stopped.

This paragraph has accurate and concise information about Stolypin's reforms. There is a slight loss of focus in the second sentence, but it becomes relevant again reasonably quickly. The problem with the paragraph is that it does not explain why these changes mattered so much; that peasant unrest had reached such unprecedented levels in 1905 that the Tsar had been persuaded to buy them off and was now trying to win them (or at least the strongest elements of them) over to his side to avoid a repeat. The link between more grain production and industrial growth is not made either, so the opportunities to use this knowledge have not been taken. The final sentence does link back to the question, but the reason for the importance of the reforms needs reiterating.

The conclusion does sum up the results but the judgement is weak – the reason for choosing the Duma as the main result is not justified and then the final sentence leaves the answer open again. It would have been better to support this choice with a clear reason.

This response has several good features, lifting it above level 3.

- The question has been understood and tackled fairly directly.
- The supporting evidence is certainly accurate and has been selected not poured out indiscriminately.
- It is clearly structured and the focus stays mainly on the question.

Two things keep it down within the level: firstly, the relevance of several points is not fully explained (which is highlighted in the weak conclusion) and secondly, the range of results examined is limited in scope. To improve further, the student would need to expand their answer, to include more depth and development.

Overall, this answer achieves a low level 4 and would gain **19 marks**.

Grade A student answer

For the educated middle classes in Russia the creation of the Duma was the most important result of the 1905 Revolution because it gave them a say in governing Russia for the first time, something they had been demanding for years, even though radical liberals complained that it didn't go far enough. However, the peasantry was affected much more by Stolypin's land reforms so, for them, this was the most important outcome. For the protesting industrial workers the short-term result was entirely negative as they felt the full force of Tsarist repression when their uprisings were crushed; although later on some of the workers benefitted from the reforms affecting education and health insurance. So, the importance of the results of the revolution varied according to which group is being looked at and the Duma was by no means the only important result of 1905.

Before the Duma was created the Tsar had ruled as an autocrat, taking advice from his ministers and the Church as he saw fit but with no restrictions on his power. After 1905, Russia had some kind of constitution for the very first time and people had the right to vote for delegates to represent them in a national parliament. Political parties were legalised and the amount of censorship reduced, so there was a lot more political freedom in general. This in itself makes the creation of the Duma really important as a change in the Russian political system.

However, in reality its importance was lessened by the 1906 Fundamental Law, which laid down numerous restrictions on the Duma's actual powers. This law made it clear that Russia was still really an autocracy because the Tsar had the power to appoint his ministers without consulting the Duma and had the right to rule by decree when the Duma was not in session. Since he had the right to dissolve it when he wanted, this meant he would not be prevented from doing what he wanted even if the Duma objected. The Fundamental Law also gave the Tsar the right to alter the electoral system, which is what he did after the second Duma, and because of this both the third and fourth Dumas were far less critical of the government than the first two had been – these had both made radical demands which the Tsar had no intention of listening to, so the new electoral law restricted the vote to the richest 30% of the male population. ☞

The introduction shows understanding that the answer cannot be clear-cut since different groups had different priorities and it broadens things out beyond the stated consequence. It is clear that the candidate has understood the complexity of the question, the line of argument has been established and the structure of the rest of the answer is clearly going to be an examination of the impact of 1905 on the middle classes, the peasantry and the urban workers in turn.

It is good practice to deal with the stated factor (in this case, consequence) first and clear factual details of the changes have been selected to do this. Contrasting the situation before 1905 with the changes afterwards has allowed the answer to highlight the most significant changes. The final sentence makes the point explicit by referring back to the wording of the question. The paragraph would have been made even more effective by reinforcing the theoretical value of the changes; pointing out that since the *zemstva* had enabled the middle classes to help run things at a regional level, they now had the chance to contribute constructively at a national level as well. Also, since every section of society, including the non-Russian minorities, now had some means of legally airing their views, Tsarism ought to have had brighter future prospects.

This shows the limitations of the stated factor concisely, without getting bogged down in unnecessary detail. A less-controlled answer might have gone into detail about the complexities of the electoral colleges and the various property qualifications, but it is enough to show the extent to which the new franchise limited participation. However, it would have been better if the key dates of the Dumas and electoral changes had been supplied, with perhaps some additional comment about the length of time the third and fourth Dumas sat compared to the first two.

Nevertheless, despite these restrictions on the amount of democracy being introduced, the Octobrists welcomed it because they had been frightened that events in 1905 were drifting out of control and they feared revolution more than they disliked Tsarism; even the more radical Kadets could see it as a first step in the right direction. The third and fourth Dumas passed some limited but useful legislation concerning the army, they backed the increased spending on primary education and they approved the reduction in powers of the land captains, all of which suggests that the parliamentary system was settling down. Although when the war broke out in 1914 the Duma was sidelined by the Tsar, it is significant that when he abdicated in 1917 it was the remnants of the Duma, in the form of the Provisional Government, that took over, which shows that the new parliament had taken root.

However, while the Duma was the most important consequence of 1905 for politically-conscious liberals, for the peasants it was the land reforms that came out of the revolution that mattered most. Peasant unrest had reached such alarming levels that the Tsar had decided to buy them off by scrapping redemption payments early and then Stolypin's land reforms continued this attempt to win them over. Stolypin had called it the 'wager on the strong', meaning he was going to support the strongest elements in the peasantry and help them break free from the restrictions of the *mir* and give them a stake in society so that they would not want to participate in any future disorder because they would have too much to lose. His package of reforms meant that peasants could leave the *mir* more easily and borrow money at low interest rates from the Land Bank in order to migrate eastwards to open up Siberia or invest in new machinery. The *mir* had been holding back change because it was dominated by old conservatives but now it was possible for progressive peasants to buy more land and farm it as a single unit, or leave altogether for somewhere new.

Although it took time for these initiatives to take effect, there were some impressive results and by 1914 about 50% of peasants owned their own land, compared to only 20% in 1906. Grain production had also gone up over 30% in this period and Lenin had commented from exile that if things carried on at this rate there would never be a revolution in Russia. Not only would Russia be stabilised by the emergence of a more loyal ☞

This paragraph sums up the importance of the stated factor to the middle class by using selected evidence to demonstrate why they saw it as the way forward. The final point about 1917 is good because it shows understanding in a thematic way; weaker candidates see 1914 as a dividing line after which everything changed, whereas there was continuity as well in some things.

An even better answer might go on to discuss briefly why the Duma was vital to the Tsar. Merely conceding it in principle had been enough to split the liberal opposition and also secured him vital loans from democratic France, so that he would still be able to finance his policies – even if the Duma was not in session because he had dissolved it.

This is an effective way to introduce the next part of the answer, by linking it back to the previous point. It then establishes the key factual details about how the peasantry were affected by the new reforms that 1905 had forced the government to make. Again, the factual support is concise and selective – this is certainly not a candidate indiscriminately off-loading all their knowledge. The final comment explains why the dismantling of the *mir* was an important result.

peasantry, but also the increased grain yields would allow the growing cities to be better fed and increased exports would buy the industrial machinery that Russia's factories needed. Taking all this into account, the land reforms were even more important than the creation of the Duma, since they affected more people and had economic as well as political consequences.

In contrast, for the industrial workers the results of 1905 were less positive. In the short term those on strike were harshly dealt with at the end of 1905, and throughout 1906 Stolypin was busy ensuring that rebels were brought under control, as several thousand death sentences were carried out. Furthermore, the franchise changes of 1906 meant fewer workers had the vote and so the Duma became less relevant to them. The expansion of primary education and the start of health and accident insurance were minor improvements that eventually came out of 1905, but the overall attitude of the Tsar to the urban workers remained hostile, as the massacre of the Lena goldfields strikers in 1912 highlights. Overall, therefore, the industrial workers could see few obvious changes coming as a result of 1905.

In conclusion, the most important consequence for the politically-motivated middle class was definitely the Duma, which may have been seriously restricted by the 1906 Fundamental Law and Nicholas' attitude towards it, but still was a significant step towards some kind of future democratic system in which the better-off professional class shared power with the old landed elite. However, the significance of this was outweighed by the land reforms because these had not only political effects in stabilising a sizeable proportion of the huge peasantry, but also the economic potential to help speed up industrial growth on which Russia's future depended. For the urban workers, the results were much more negative because the government felt strong enough to repress them if it had the middle class and the better-off peasantry on its side.

This paragraph neatly summarises the impact of Stolypin's reforms on the peasantry. The line of argument has now evolved slightly with more emphasis being put on the land issues. Using statistics in this way is useful since a clear contrast is being made. However, Lenin's comment might have been made more explicitly relevant by explaining that he feared that if the peasantry's grievances were significantly reduced, then the prospects of a successful revolution would be much slimmer since the peasantry still made up about 80% of the population.

Dividing the consequences into short-term and long-term results is a good way to show how things changed at different rates. However, this section is rather brief and could have been more effective if it had included some detail about the extent to which the later reforms actually benefitted the urban workers. Also, the link back to the political section is not taken very far and it would have been possible to comment on the repressive tactics of the *Okhrana* in trying to stop the Marxists recruiting working-class support. Just because these results involved less change and more repression does not stop them being important, which is what the question is asking about.

The conclusion sums up the argument clearly and makes a judgement, explaining the reasoning behind the preferred choice, while also acknowledging the importance of the stated consequence. 👉

The answer shows awareness of the difficulties in reaching a judgement of a complex situation where different groups experienced different outcomes from the 1905 Revolution.

The student has tackled question directly, the full time period has been covered and has included a range of relevant factors (consequences).

They have made clear links between the various consequences.

The answer is clearly structured, looking at three different social groups in turn and with frequent references to the wording of the question, particularly at the end of paragraphs.

The factual support is accurate and precise, and is always used to support a point, rather than being included for its own sake. Analysis is sustained throughout – there are no descriptive passages.

It is written in a confident style, and a final judgement was reached, which is supported by the evidence selected.

However, while the depth is good, the answer would ideally cover a slightly wider range of results. A paragraph on the way 1905 affected the Tsar's attitude to ruling Russia would have given a more complete picture. Examiners are aware of time constraints, though, and a strong level 5 does not have to include everything. The key quality is to use what you know effectively, which this answer does.

Overall, this answer achieves a level 5 and would gain **28 marks**.

Page numbers in *italic* show entry in an artwork.

1905 Revolution 22–7

A

agriculture, increase in production 32, 33, 62
Alexander II, Tsar (1855–81) 6, 7, 16
Alexander III, Tsar (1881–94) 7–9, 16
Alexandra, Tsarina (1872–1918) 36
All-Russian Congress of Soviets 44, *44*, *51*
anarchism, definition 19
Anti-Semitism
     fuels the Bund (1897) 16
     May Laws (1882) 9
     pogroms (1880s) 9
     pogroms (1905) 29
     Witte 15
Army
     anti-war feeling 41
     casualties (1914–17) 36
     repression 7, 35
     Tsarist regime 27, 38–9
Army mutinies (1905) *25*
autocracy, definition of 6

B

Bakunin, Michael 16
Baltic Provinces (Estonia, Latvia and Lithuania) 9, *25*, 47, 52, *53*, 54
Barmine, Alexander, 'Revolution betrayed' 62
Black Earth region 4, 11, 14, *25*, 62
Black Hundreds (1905–6) 29
'Black Repartition', populism 16, *17*
'Bloody Sunday' (1905) *22*, 24, *25*, *26*, *26*
Bolsheviks
     1917–8 50–1
     1917–24 66–7, *66*
     Bolshevik-Menshevik split 21
     Democratic Centralists 61
     July days 44–5
     Kornilov affair 44
     Kronstadt revolt 60

'Peace, Bread and Land' slogan 43
     Relationship with the Church 63
     Workers' Opposition 61, 67
     see also October/November Revolution, Civil War, NEP
bourgeoisie, new social class 20
Brest-Litovsk, Treaty of (1918) 52, *53*, 55, 56, 59
Bukharin, Nikolai (1888–1938) 66, 67
Bunge, N.K., Finance Minister (1881–86) 14
bureaucracy (civil service) 7, 38–9

C

capitalism, historical stage 20
censorship 7, 9
     and the arts 64
Cheka 67
     grain requisitions 57, 67
     Lenin 59
     murder of Tsar and family 51
     'Red Terror' 51
     see also GPU
Chernov, Victor (1873–1952) 18, 18–9, 35, 41, 59
Combat Organisation (terrorists) 19, 24
Committee of Members of the Constituent Assembly *Komuch* 52
communism, historical stage 20
Constituent Assembly *41*, 43, 50, 52
     1917 election results 47, *47*, 48–9
Constitutional Democratic Party *see* Kadets
constitutional monarchy, definition 18
Czech Legion 54, 55, *56*

D

Denikin, General Anton
     Armed Forces of Southern Russia (AFSR) 54, 55, *56*
     unpopular land and nationalism aims 59
Duma 26, 30–1

February/March Revolution 38, *38*, 39
     October Manifesto 30
Durnovo, P.N., Interior Minister 28, 35

E

Emancipation Statutes (1861) 6

F

famine
     (1891–2) 14, 16
     (1921) 62
February/March Revolution 38, *38*, 39, 47
feudalism, historical stage 20
Finland, appeal to refuse taxes *25*, 31, 47, 52, *53*
Franco-Russian alliance (1894) 13
Fundamental Laws
     (1832) 30
     (1906) 30, 31, 34, 35, 38
     Article 87 31, 35

G

Gapon, Father, leads march 24, 26
Georgia, serious unrest (1905) *25*, 59
Glavlit (Directorate for Literature and Publishing) 64
gold standard 14
GPU 63
Great Reforms (1850s) 6–7, 8
'Greens', freelance peasant forces 54, *56*
Guchkov, Alexander (1862–1936), Octobrist leader *17*, 36, 39, 41, 59

I

Imperial State Council (1906) 30, 31
industrial development
     1881–1914 12–5, *13*, 34, 35
     'crisis of modernisation' 22
     obstacles to 4, 12, *32*
     and Witte 14–5
     see also War Communism, NEP
inflation, definition 37, *37*

K

Kadets (Constitutional Democratic Party) (radical liberals) *17*, 18, *25*, 27, 31, 36, 39, 50
Kamenev, L.B.(1883–1936), Bolshevik leader 42, 46, 66
Kaplan, Fanya, attempts assassination of Lenin 51
Kerensky, Alexander (1881–1970) 39, 41, 45, *46*, 59
Kolchak, Admiral
    Siberian White army 53, 55, *56*
    unpopular land and nationalism aims 59
Kollontai, Alexandra, Commissar for Social Welfare 61
Komsomol (Young Communists) 63
Kornilov, General Lavr (1870–1918), orders advance on Petrograd 45, 49, 52
Kronstadt sailors
    1905 Revolution 25
    anti-Bolshevik mutiny (1921) 60, 67
    October/November Revolution 1917 44, 45, 46

L

land captains replace *zemstva* 8
'Land and Liberty' organisation, populist 16, *17*
land reforms 32, 33, *34*, 38, 41
land transfer (1861), redemption payments 10, 11, 38
Lenin, Vladimir Ilyich Ulyanov (1870–1924) 42–3, 66, 67
    'April Theses' 42–3, 44, 48
    chairs Sovnarkom 50
    death (1924) 62, *66*
    fails to seize power in July 1917 44, 48
    formation of the Bolshevik Party 21
    July Days 44
    leadership role in Civil War 59
    NEP Russia 60–3, *65*
    October/November Revolution 1917 46, 47, 48
    the Russian Social Democratic and Labour Party 17, *17*, 21
    and Stalin 66
    The Development of Capitalism (1896) 21
    totalitarianism 65
    What Is To Be Done? (1902) 21
liberals *see* Kadets (Constitutional Democratic Party); Octobrists
Liberation of Labour Group (Marxists) *17*, 21
local government reform, *zemstva* 6, 8
Loris-Melikov, Count Mikhail (Interior Minister) 8
Lvov, Prince 39, 41, 45

M

Martov, Juli (Tsederbaum) (1873–1923)
    leads Mensheviks *17*, 21, 59
    forms RSDLP 21
Marx, Karl (1818–83)
    Das Kapital (1861) 20
    dictatorship of the proletariat 50
    The Communist Manifesto (1848) 20
    theory of history 20, 42
Marxists
    Bolsheviks q.v. *17*
    industrial workers seen as key 19
    lengthy process to communism 42
    Liberation of Labour Group *17*, 21
    Mensheviks q.v. *17*
    Russian Social Democratic Labour Party 16, *17*, 21
Maximalists (populists) *17*, 19
Mensheviks *17*, 39, 40, 42, 48, 50, 63
middle classes 5, 15, 18
    anti-government feeling 22, *26*, 39
    Congress of *zemstvo* members *25*
    support Provisional Government 40
Milyukov, Paul (1859–1943), Foreign Minister *17*, 36, 39, 41, 59
mir (village commune) 11, 16, 19, 32
Moscow
    armed uprising 25, 27
    Bolshevik uprising 47
    clashes with strikers (1921) 60
    engineering and textile industries 12, *13*
    population halved 57
    threatened by Whites 55

N

Naval mutinies (1905) *25*
New Economic Policy 62–5
Nicholas II, Tsar (1894–1917) 7, 15, 26, 27, 30, 34–6, 38, 39, 51

O

October Manifesto (1905) 26–7, 30, 34
October/November Revolution 46–9
    uprising or coup 49, *49*
Octobrists (moderate liberals) *17*, 18, *25*, 27, 31, 36, 39
Okhrana 7, 15, 24, 35, 51, 67
opposition to Tsarism fails 35

P

Pale of Settlement, pogroms (1880s) 9
Peasant Land Bank (1883) 11, 33
peasantry
    increasing discontent 11, 22, *26*
    strip system 10, 11, *32*, 32, 33, *34*
    village commune or *mir* 11, 16, 19, 32, 33
peasantry after 1905
    merciless intimidation by army 28, 29
    violence by Black Hundreds 29
peasantry and war 36, 37, 39, 56, 57, 60, 61

Index

Peasants' Union (1905) *25*

'People's Will' revolutionaries 7, 16

Petrograd
Alexandra controls affairs 36
anti-war demonstrations 41
clashes with strikers (1921) 60
garrison mutiny (February) 38, *38*
garrison mutiny (July) 44
militant trade unions grow 43
'ministerial leapfrog' 36
soviet established 38
strikes and demonstrations 37, *38*
Winter Palace stormed 46
workers' control of factories 43, 57

Petrograd Soviet *38*, 39
'Appeal to All the Peoples of the World' 41
mobilises to defend Petrograd 45
support of soldiers and factory workers 40

Petropavlovsk Resolution 60

Pipes, Richard, *The Russian Revolution* 10, 26, 44, 49

Plehve, V.K. (1846–1904), assassinated 15, *22*, 24, 26

Plekhanov, G.V., founds Liberation of Labour Group *17*, 21

Pobedonostev, Konstantin (1827–1907) 8

Poland 9, 12, *13*
conquered by Germany (1914) 36
declares independence 47
general strike and demonstrations (1905–6) *25*
Russo-Polish War (1920–21) 55
surrender of 52, *53*

population growth 4–5, 11

populists
the 'Black Repartition' 16, *17*
'Land and Liberty' organisation 16, *17*
Maximalists *17*, 19
the 'People's Will' 16

see also Socialist Revolutionary Party

Port Arthur, Siege of (1904–5) 23, *23*, 24

Portsmouth, Treaty of (1905) 24, 26

Potemkin (battleship) 25

Pravda (newspaper) 67

press freedom ended 50

proletariat 20, 50

Provisional Government
aims for all-round peace 43
April crisis 40–1
growing unpopularity 42–3
lack of real power 39, 40
plans for political future 41, *41*
policies mocked by Lenin 49
refuses to sanction land seizures 43
weaknesses and failures 49

Putilov engineering complex 13, *22*, *38*, 59

R

Railway workers' strike (1905) 25

Rasputin, Grigory (1872–1916) *starets* and healer 36, 37

Red Army 67
Civil War 54, 55, 58, *59*
peasants' revolt 60, 67
requisitioning grain 57

'Red Guards' formed 43, 46

republic, definition of 18

revolutionary defensism 41

Riasanovsky, Nicholas, *A History of Russia* 36

Riga, Treaty of (1921) 55

Russian Civil War (1918–20) 54–5, *56*
armament manufacturing capacity 58
differing manpower pools 58, *59*
reasons for Bolshevik victory 58–9, *58*

Russian Orthodox Church
attacks by Bolsheviks 63
identified with Tsarism 5, 7, 9
separated from the state 51, 63
'show trials' of churchmen 63

Russian Social Democratic Labour Party (Marxists) 16, *17*, 21

Russian Socialist Federated Soviet Republic, institutions *51*

Russification 9

Russo-Japanese War (1904–5) *22*, 23–4, *26*

Rykov, A.I., heads *Vesenkha* 57

S

St Petersburg
engineering and textile industries 12, *13*
name changed to Petrograd 36

St Petersburg Soviet, formed and disbanded (1905) *25*, 27

Secret political police *see Okhrana*

Separatist movements, non-Russian minorities 54

serfs, emancipation of (1861) 7, 10

Service, Robert, *Did Lenin lead to Stalin?* 65

Shlyapnikov, Alexander, Commissar for Labour 61

Smith, S.A., *The Russian Revolution: Short Introduction* 22

socialism, definition of 19

Socialist Revolutionary Party (SRs) (populists) 17, 18–9, 22
April Crisis 1917 40, 41
Constituent Assembly elections 1917 47, 49
Combat Organisation (terrorists) 19
Komuch 52
split 48
suppression 50, 63

Sovdepia (Bolshevik area)
economic problems 56
food rationing 57
internal passports introduced 57
workers' councils scrapped 57

Sovnarkom (People's Commissars) 46, 49, 50, *51*
Decrees seek public support 50
sidelined 66

Stalin, Joseph (1879–1953)
    General Secretary 66
    Sovnarkom Commissar 42, 50
Stolypin, P.A (1862–1911)
    assassination 32, 33
    Chairman Council of Ministers 19, 28
    countryside repression 28, 35
    Duma rejected 31, 34, 35
    emergency court-martials 28
    land reforms 32–3, 35, 38
    plans for more *zemstva* fail 31

T
Temporary Laws (1881–1905 and later) 8
terrorism
    definition of 19
    in rural areas 28
    state 51, 59, 65
totalitarian state, characteristics 65, *65*
trade unions, legalised (1905) 38
Trans-Siberian Railway (1905) 15
Transcaucasian separatists, Armenian, Georgian and Azerbaijani 54, 59
Trotsky, Leon (Bronstein) (1879–1940)
    arrest 27
    Brest-Litovsk 52
    defeats North-Western Army 55
    leads St Petersburg Soviet *25*, 35, 42
    Military Revolutionary Committee 46, *46*
    'scissors crisis' 62
    seizure of power 46, 48
    Sovnarkom Commissar 50
Tsarist regime
    concedes elected assembly 26
    October Manifesto 26
    retains powers under Fundamental Laws 30
    ruthless fight for survival 35
    suppresses Soviet 27
    survives 1905 revolution 27

Tsushima, Battle of (1905) 23, *23*, 24
Tukhachevsky, General Mikhail 59

U
Ukraine, declares independence 9, 47, 52, *53*, 59
Union of Liberation (Liberal) *17*, *22*
Union of Russian Social Democrats Abroad 21
Union of Unions (1905) *25*
universities 7, 9, 16, *25*
urban unrest
    apalling conditions 16, 22, *26*
    shortages and high prices *32*, 56, 60
    trade union rights lost under War Communism 60
    workers return to villages 57
Uvarov, S.S., 'Orthodoxy, Autocracy, Nationality' 29

V
Vesenkha (Supreme Council of National Economy) 57
Volkogonov, Dmitri, Trotsky's biographer 48
Vyshnegradsky, I.A., Finance Minister (1886–1892), tough financed policies 14, 16

W
War (1914–17)
    'Brusilov offensive' (1916) 36
    defeat and mismanagement 35, 36
    Eastern Front offensive (June 1917) 44
War Communism
    coercive measures 57, 59
    hostility to 60
    grain requisition 57, 61, 62
    'one-man' management 57, 61
Whites 54, 55, 58, 59
Witte, Sergei (1849–1915)
    Finance Minister
        agriculture modernisation 12
        adopts gold standard 14

high import duties 14, 15
political and strategic aims 14
opposition to his reforms 15
railway construction 15
technical schools and institutes 15
Prime Minister
    advises political concessions 26, 35
    Nicholas dismisses (1906) 27
    suppresses St Petersburg Soviet 27
    condemns Black Hundreds 29
women and the family 64
working class
    armed uprising in Moscow suppressed *25*, 27
    Empire-wide general strike *25*, 27
    growth of 5, 15
    labour unrest (1890s) 16, 22, *26*
    Railway workers' strike (1905) *25*
    St Petersburg Soviet 25
working class and war
    food in short supply 37, 43
    rampant inflation 37, 39, 43
    strikes and demonstrations 37
Wrangel, Baron, Armed Forces of Southern Russia (AFSR) 54

Y
Yudenich, General Nikolai, North-Western Army 54, 55, *56*

Z
Zemstvo representatives
    call for democratic assembly *25*
    called 'dreamers' by Nicholas *26*
Zemstvo Statute (1890) 9
Zinoviev, Grigori (1883–1936) 42, 46